WALTER CAMP

ON THE SIDE LINES

WALTER CAMP

THE FATHER OF
AMERICAN FOOTBALL

AN AUTHORIZED BIOGRAPHY

BY

HARFORD POWEL, JR.

WITH AN INTRODUCTION BY
E. K. HALL
Chairman, American Intercollegiate
Football Rules Committee

With Illustrations

BOOKS FOR LIBRARIES PRESS
FREEPORT, NEW YORK

First Published 1926
Reprinted 1970

STANDARD BOOK NUMBER:
8369-5473-4

LIBRARY OF CONGRESS CATALOG CARD NUMBER:
70-126246

PRINTED IN THE UNITED STATES OF AMERICA

TO

"MRS. WALTER"

EVERY MAN WHO PLAYED FOOTBALL FOR YALE,
WHILE WALTER CAMP WAS COACH,
WILL KNOW WHY THIS BOOK
IS DEDICATED TO HER

INTRODUCTION

By Edward K. Hall

Chairman, American Intercollegiate Football Rules Committee

THE writer of this book tells me that he has written it primarily for the schoolboys of America. He has done well to keep them uppermost in his mind, for they had no truer and no more understanding friend than Walter Camp.

As a boy himself, he was just naturally all boy, a typical American boy full of spirit and dash, keen for play and competition, and reveling in wholesome sport and contest. As a man, he never lost the boy's point of view. His interest in boys was unbounded, and his understanding of them was as sympathetic as it was complete. The schoolboys of America have for years regarded Walter Camp as their great friend. They will continue to do so for years to come, and they have a right to. For he has not only given them the greatest of all their sports, American Rugby Football, but has taught them how to play it, and how to keep fit. He has pointed out how these battles of the gridiron help to develop the qualities so essential to success in later life.

Above all, he has taught them by both spoken and written word, by precept and example, the finest ideals of American sportsmanship.

The American boy who has not read *Danny Fists* by Walter Camp has missed as much as the English boy who has failed to read *Tom Brown's School-Days*.

The Sportsmanship Brotherhood defines the true sportsman as one who : —

Plays the game for his side;

Keeps to the rules;

Keeps a stout heart in defeat;

Keeps faith with his comrades;

Keeps himself fit;

Keeps his temper;

Keeps modest in victory;

Keeps a sound soul, a clean mind, and a healthy body.

I have never known a man who exemplified the sportsman's code better than Camp.

In almost a lifelong association with him I never heard him speak unkindly either of or to another person and I cannot imagine Walter Camp doing a mean act. More than once I have seen him face the bitterest disappointment with a smile on his face that was a joy to see and with a fortitude that was literally inspiring. Time and again I have watched him and marvelled as he held his temper under conditions that would have tested the temper of a saint. His fairness toward those whose views he opposed and his consideration for the feelings of others were never failing.

He was the hard-fighting, clean-hitting, straight-shooting type of a sportsman that commands the respect and admiration of his opponents and the affection of his comrades.

The American schoolboy will welcome this book as his own. He will be a better sportsman for having read it and he will be a better citizen. He will become better acquainted with his great and good friend Walter Camp who for generations to come will be remembered as one of the finest of America's sportsmen.

CONTENTS

CONTENTS

ILLUSTRATIONS

WALTER CAMP

I

THE ROUND BLACK RUBBER FOOTBALL

THIS man surely said to himself in boyhood, as most boys have said before him : " I have only one life to lead, and I want to get out of it as much fun and as many rewards as I can."

If he took stock of himself in a mirror, — and what boy has not, — he saw a tall, loosely knit, slender boy, with no marked muscular development nor depth of chest, but with a pair of exceedingly bright and even burning dark eyes. Nobody who ever looked Walter Camp in the face can forget those eyes. Men with eyes like that are rare, and they indicate a spirit that commands other men.

But before Walter Camp could command others, he had to learn to command himself. He had great advantages. His mental equipment was far above the ordinary. He had a superbly controlled memory — there was never a time in his life when he would fail to repeat accurately any poem that struck his fancy, or the substance of any important letter or conversation. A powerful memory gives its possessor a tremendous start toward all creative thinking. Upon such a foundation it is easy to build new ideas. Camp observed a great deal, remembered it all, and constantly revolved the useful parts of it in his mind. He did not doze or dream. He was either wide awake or sound asleep. And when, perhaps fifty-five years ago, he started to take stock of himself, he no doubt thought like this : —

"There is no fortune waiting for me. If I want more money than I can earn from a weekly salary, I shall have to make it. I am not naturally strong. My arm has no bulging muscle. My neck, wrists, chest, and calves are all slimmer than in most boys of my age. If I am to excel in sports, I must build myself up, and cultivate speed and agility."

He went to work so quietly at this process of building himself up that even his best chums in school — the boys who have since become Mr. Julian W. Curtiss and Mr. Walter Jennings — cannot recall precisely what it was he did. I once asked him. He admitted, smilingly, that he was an undermuscled, gawky boy. He said he had planned a few body-building exercises for himself, but he did not describe them definitely. He could be more definite than most men when he cared to be, so it was clear that he did not wish to talk in detail about those personal things. That was another characteristic of him. Few distinguished men ever went through life, in modern America, with such sparse use of the first person singular pronoun.

But I have a very clear picture of what he must have done. As a school-teacher's son, his parents had no money to give him for visits to western ranches, or for the long sea voyages that were once regularly prescribed for underdeveloped boys. Walter Camp must have had his own private gymnasium in his small bedroom in his parents' home. He must have bent forward and back and sideways, patiently, half a hundred times each morning. He must have risen dozens of times a day on his toes, before the steel-like tendons in his legs gave him the superb power and balance that marked his football running later on. He must have inhaled deeply and regularly, before that thin chest of his became deep. He took long runs on the roads around New Haven. Physical development is not a gift. It comes because a man has worked for it, somehow. Theodore Roosevelt paid the price for it in one way, Walter Camp in another, Abraham Lincoln and George Washington in still another. Lincoln owed his powerful body to his early days as an axe-man and pioneer. Washington developed his magnificent physique by breaking new trails in the wilderness. It makes no difference which powerful man you call to mind — behind them all is some kind of physical training and some memory of regular daily exercise in the formative years. No man develops strong muscles and tendons by sitting at a desk and wishing for strength.

Walter Camp used to grin appreciatively at the stories told in the biographies of famous Americans.

"Look at James J. Hill," he said, "a great grizzly bear of a man who gained his enormous physical strength in railroad construction camps. Look at the man who founded the Vanderbilt family, a sailboat man, accustomed to hoisting sail and handling the tiller in any weather, as part of his ferry business. Collis P. Huntington was a farm hand. Marshall Field grew up on a farm. All were accustomed to hard outdoor labor of some kind, and thus had advantages denied to many of our younger men to-day. The sons and grandsons of men like these are city born and bred. Body-building toil has gone out of their lives."

Camp, himself, was reared in a home full of comfort if not of luxury. He never did any manual labor except household chores. His mother, among her other housewifely talents, was a famous baker of chocolate cake. But Walter could always refuse a second helping, just as in manhood he could always refuse a cigarette or a second chocolate éclair. He was always, eternally, training himself and rejoicing quietly in every physical victory he won. He learned to get much more fun out of self-denial than out of indulgence. Those six or seven strokes in a round of golf by which, at sixty-five, he regularly beat men of forty and fifty, were far more satisfactory to him than the six or seven cigarettes he paid for them.

He was a born competitor, a man who delighted to win. Too many people slack-wittedly imagine the true sportsman to be "a good loser." The true sportsman is, of course, preëminently a good winner; a man who disdains all small and crooked tricks, but who spares no pains to achieve victory by all honorable means, including, most of all, a thorough preparation. Walter Camp never went into a match of any kind, nor let any team he coached go into a match, without having done everything legitimately possible to assure victory. No detail was too small for him. He became the kind of golfer who will diligently practise a single stroke until he masters it — on a golf course if possible, or in the back garden if no golf course is available, or on the hearthrug if there is no back garden. No detail in any game was too small for Camp. If one less cocktail on Friday evening means one less stroke in a round of golf on the following Saturday, Camp was the kind of man who cheerfully leaves that cocktail in the shaker. Camp had always a little more wind, a little less fat, than his opponent; his eye was a little clearer and his hand a little steadier. That little is often the difference between victory and defeat.

So our first picture of Walter Camp is that of a boy trying patiently to build a slim body to fighting pitch. He attended a splendid school, Hopkins Grammar, in New Haven. This school is older than Yale College. Its students were a *corps d'élite*. Fathers sent their boys there from many other cities. There were no dormitories. The boys lived in rooming houses all over town. Think of that, you fathers who have come to regard the magnificent dormitories at such modern schools as Exeter, or Hotchkiss, or St. George's, or Middlesex, as mere necessities for your sons. Walter Jennings remembers how his father took him to New Haven, found him a room in a boarding house, and left him with the parting admonition to be good and not get into trouble. Whether a fourteen-year-old boy could be trusted nowadays to bear himself with discretion in a strange city, under similar circumstances, is a matter of opinion. The Hopkins boys managed to do it. It is to the credit of the spirit of Hopkins School and of its principal, Dr. Samuel Johnson, that the numerous opportunities for dissipation were not accepted. While Camp was in school, William L. Cushing, an old Yale oarsman, became head master. The boys adored him, and the discipline of the school was strengthened by his example.

Walter Camp lived in his parents' home. He respected his school-teacher father, from whom he inherited his keen intellect, but he was not subjected to sharp parental discipline. He could have lounged around street corners at night, had he wished, and smoked cigarettes and drunk beer. But he did not choose. He was a competitor, through and through. He wanted to excel at both studies and sports. Take studies first. Here is

WALTER CAMP AS A SCHOOLBOY

the standing of his class at Hopkins, for the month
ending February 24, 1874 : —

James M. Hoppin .	5.00	Alfred E. Hooker .	4.36
Waldo Hutchins, Jr.	5.00	Frank A. Kellogg .	4.30
Wilson C. Wheeler .	5.00	Charles F. Bliss . .	4.17
Walter Camp . .	4.86	Willis Benner . .	4.12
Charles P. Wurts, Jr.	4.85	George J. Augur .	3.99
Wm. P. Hotchkiss .	4.79	Rufus Waple . . .	3.99
Colin M. McKenzie	4.75	William H. Moseley	3.83
Henry Hine . . .	4.74	Charles A. Baker .	3.75
John A. March . .	4.72	Oliver W. Dye . .	3.75
Edward W. Knevals	4.69	S. Charles Metzger .	3.65
Frank H. Wheeler .	4.58	George P. Fisher .	3.46
William G. Daggett	4.57	Wilson H. Clark .	3.40
Fred H. Benton . .	4.52	Stewart Sumner . .	3.39
Walter Hall . . .	4.48	John E. Brainard .	3.31
Edward Graves . .	4.46	James Degnan . .	3.15
Walter Jennings . .	4.40	Edgar S. Porter . .	2.97
		Edward H. Genung	2.36

Ten months later, as shown by the report published on December 1, 1874, there was no appre-
ciable difference. Hoppin, Hutchins, and Wheeler
were still leading the class, each with a miraculous,
perfect record. Lawrence Wilkinson, a new boy,
had 4.92. Walter Camp followed with an improved
standing of 4.87. The other thirty-four boys in
the class were rated below him.

And, if you pass over a year and look at the class
record on December 14, 1875, when the boys were
seniors, you will find Camp ranked sixth in a class
now totaling thirty-five boys. Evidently, he was

not then — and was not going to be — the kind of
athlete who takes a certain warped satisfaction in
poor scholastic marks.   There have been too many
such boys in our schools and colleges.   In the days
when college football players prided themselves on
their toughness it was unfashionable to have, or
at least, to seem to have, any brain at all.
Grinds, or polers, or digs, as they are variously
called at the colleges, are seldom popular men.
This is because they have overdone the appearance
of being students, as much as football men used to
overdo the appearance of being toughs.   But there
has come about, in the past fifteen years, a revalua-
tion of brains and mental earnestness.   The newspaper sports writers have helped, by making it
clear to boys everywhere that a professional baseball player like Rogers Hornsby for instance, or Ty
Cobb, or Eddie Collins, is valuable to his team not
because he is tough, but because he is intelligent.
Such a man has brains, sharpens them by study
and observation, and uses them in every game.
He is a "smart" player.   So in football have such
modern players as Friedman and Dooley and Buell
and Richeson come to be appreciated by the spectators, and by boys everywhere, because they are
first of all intelligent.   Dooley, the Dartmouth
quarterback, actually dared to write and publish
poetry of serious lyrical value, even though he was
also making the most remarkable forward passes
ever seen on any field.   These two things are not

incompatible. Thirty years ago they would have been thought so. The idea that a great halfback could have attained and held a scholastic rating of better than 85 per cent would have been regarded by most undergraduates as preposterous. They would have preferred to think of the halfback as a lazy, jovial halfwit — a man who could hardly write his name, and who never read so much as the front page of a newspaper.

All that has changed for the better, and the college athlete of to-day — if he has any regard for popularity — carefully avoids seeming to be either a rowdy or a dunce. Walter Camp was fifty years ahead of his time in that respect. Men who went to school with him remember him as an earnest student. His geniality was natural and not assumed. It would have been impossible to regard him as a dig; but his schoolmates had every reason to know that he labored faithfully at his books. Each of them remembers another significant thing about him. He was the only boy at Hopkins who had a football, and who delighted in kicking it around at recess time. At eleven o'clock each morning, Camp was the first boy to rush out on the playground, with an old round black rubber football in his hands.

Put one thing firmly out of your mind — any lingering memory you may have of *Tom Brown's School-Days*. That great book describes school-boy life in England so well that it almost seems to describe schoolboy life everywhere. Rugby, by the middle of the past century, was the home of football. It was played strenuously under consistent rules. The great match of the year was the School House against the rest of the school. Under a different set of rules it was played at Eton. But those were English schools, and to imagine that football was also played in American schools is to imagine that we also played cricket and fives. The great American game at that time was baseball, and it was practically the only American game. Outdoor sports at Hopkins Grammar School, for instance, were simple and not "organized." The present ideas about coaches, and successful seasons, and athletic policies, were unknown. Baseball and running races were about all the sports the boys had. However, Yale was not far from Hopkins, and in Yale, all through the seventies, the seeds of modern intercollegiate athletic competition were germinating fast. The Hopkins boys of those days still remember how they looked up to the Yale oarsmen and baseball players, and hoped to be numbered among them in their turn.

Many a Yale undergraduate, strolling home from the diamond or the boathouse, must have looked casually at the Hopkins boys as they played ball on their own grounds. In the mind of such an Olympian these young chaps were hardly worth a thought. There's a natural baseball player, though — that lithe young fellow, Curtiss. So

perhaps ruminated one of the Yale athletes, looking over the street at the Hopkins lads as they
played their quarrelsome and informal game, un-
supervised by any teacher or coach.

But what about that thin, tall boy of fourteen
with the round black rubber ball? Did anyone
pay him the tribute of a glance, as he stood a little
apart from the scrub baseball game, kicking his
ball high and trying to lure Curtiss or Jennings into
kicking it back again? Football in America was
an outlaw game, a sort of town game, old and dis-
reputable. Twenty or thirty boys and men, craving hard exercise and a free-for-all fight or rush,
might kick a football around, and even try to rush
it through another mob of equal size and motley-
ness. There was a football team at Yale and at
some of the other colleges; and the Canadians were
becoming proficient at the game, under English
rules. But the game was not in favor at most
American colleges, and few people cared to see it
played. Baseball and rowing and running were
the gentlemen's games.

Pass on, Yale undergraduate, and do not give the
schoolboy with the round black rubber ball another
thought. All he is doing is planting a seed which,
before you are dead, will have blossomed into a
hundred immense bowls and stadiums; will have
begun to pay all the expenses of all the other college
sports; will have made even college baseball into
virtually a minor sport; will be attracting millions

of spectators on every Saturday of every autumn ; and will have set any schoolboy's heart pounding at the slightest chance to see Edgar Poe play, or Edward Mahan, or Ben Friedman, or Red Grange.

This is what Walter Camp is preparing for America — but he does not realize it himself. He is wondering, audibly, why some of his mates won't quit baseball for a few minutes and help him kick his old black rubber ball around.

II

THE WISH TO EXCEL

THE outlines of Walter Camp's life are so simple
that they can be given in thirty lines. He was
born in New Haven on April 7, 1859. His parents
were Leverett L. Camp and Ellen Cornwall Camp.
His earliest American ancestor was Nicholas Camp,
who came to this country in 1630 from County
Essex, in England, landing at Salem, Massachu-
setts, and afterward settling in Milford, Connecticut.

Walter Camp played football and other games
with distinction at Yale for six years. From 1877
until 1925, when he died, he was a member of every
football rules committee and convention. He
married Alice Graham Sumner and was the father
of two children, Walter and Janet. He rose from
clerk to president and chairman of the New Haven
Clock Company. When Hopkins Grammar School
was reorganized, he was elected to its Board of
Trustees. During the World War he was chairman of the Athletic Department, United States
Navy Commission on Training Camp Activities.
He found time also to serve on several municipal
commissions, to write more than twenty novels,
histories, and books on sports, to edit the "Outdoor America" department in *Collier's Weekly*,

and to invent and promote the Daily Dozen system of exercise. In addition he was for thirty years
the outstanding football legislator and coach in
America, helping his college to make a winning
record that has never been equaled, and to establish
football as the most successful among all college
games. He will be remembered as the father of
American football.

So much for an outline. Like all other outlines
now so popular, it is almost worthless unless you
fill the blank spaces inside the contours. You will
observe, for instance, that he won his great national
reputation without ever changing his residence
from the small city in which he was born. Walter
Camp stayed in his home town, sure that the world
would in time come and find him there. The last
thing he ever wanted was ease and comfort. He
wanted to face the arena and make himself conspicuous in it. He wanted success, and he was willing to pay its price. But he believed, unlike a
majority of equally ambitious men, that the best
place in which to win the game of life is on the home
grounds.

If you would like a mental photograph by
which to remember Walter Camp, you will find
it in this paragraph from the preliminary notes
he wrote for the brilliant little book of practical
philosophy (not of calisthenics) called *The Daily
Dozen*, on which he was working when he
died : —

When we call a boy a thoroughbred, we know he is a boy who is high-spirited, plucky, courageous, and strong. Every boy wants to be the type that is described by these expressions. To make himself fit, he must follow the precepts of health and of morality. Every boy is eager to stand well with his fellows, to be an aid to his team in its sports, to be an individual champion, to play fair and to play well. These things are possible under a course of care and self-discipline not difficult of attainment by any youth.

But the significant sentences follow this general statement; the sentences in which Camp unconsciously described himself: —

If, however, a boy has *the wish to excel*, he takes on a contract which involves patience, self-control, persistence, and hard work. No boy or man ever made himself a leader in sports, or in life, without doing a great deal of hard work which at times seemed to be drudgery. No one comes to the top without making certain sacrifices. It is not an easy road, but it is an eminently satisfactory road, because it leads to the desired end.

These words are not the finished draft, but are the tincture or quintessence of the book that was to come. They are Camp himself, musing on the careers he had observed and on his own career. There is no sentimentality in them, no careless optimism. They have the same grim quality that you find in the writings of Robert Louis Stevenson, at his best. Camp had none of the magic of words that was Stevenson's, but he had the same conviction that the human spirit is always challenging fate, and all too often failing to make the challenge good because it is too weak or too reckless to pay the price of victory.

Camp was not among the men who say, like Theodore Roosevelt, "I've had a bully time." He had a very hard time before life began to run smoothly for him, and he remembered all about it — the bumps and bangs he received in football practice, the self-imposed torture of cross-country running before he was good enough to win a place in the quarter-mile run, the burden of captaining a college team before that team was disciplined enough to win its big games, the hardships of rigid personal economy before he went to his wife, near the end of his life, and told her that her own future was financially secure. He was no favorite child of fortune. But through all his difficulties he had in full measure "the wish to excel." And he rated his own capacity highly; he knew that life has minor rewards for the smaller men, but he did not care about them for himself. I take another paragraph from his writings. It is headed "Happiness," and reads : —

How does happiness come? What path does she tread? How may we catch this elusive creature? The preparation for the chase requires training. The chances for success lie largely in having good health.

A sick man has no time to think of anything except his own condition. A well man "rejoiceth as a strong man to run a race." Each one of us may have a different picture of happiness. The golfer who has never been under 110 strokes finishes a round, it may be, in 99 strokes. He is happy, but the 99 strokes that brought him happiness would be gall and wormwood to the scratch player. A tennis player who has never before survived the early rounds comes up to the finals and takes the runner-up's prize. And that prize makes him happy, even though he finds himself outclassed by the champion. The man who has no luck all his life in his investments wakes up some morning to find that a stock he had supposed worthless is suddenly running up in leaps and bounds, and his holdings in it may make him free from money troubles again. And he is happy. An unexpected public honor may bring happiness to one, a relief from harassing cares may bring it to another. Someone has said that mere freedom from intolerable pain is the happiness of the aged; but this would mean nothing to the youth who does not know pain. His must be an active, not a passive happiness. His must be success, victory. And these can come only through health and work beforehand.

Nothing is more characteristic of Camp than the wish to excel. He entered Yale College in September 1876, and went out promptly for a place on the famous football team of which Eugene V. Baker was captain. For three years Yale had played Association football with some minor modifications, but in the autumn of 1876 the first call

had been sounded for a new, modern form of football. Princeton issued a call for a meeting. Yale,
Harvard, and Columbia answered this call, and
their representatives met with those of Princeton at
the old Massasoit House in Springfield, Massachu-
setts. The Rugby Union rules in modified form
were adopted, an intercollegiate football association formed, and a schedule of games prepared.
Baker went back to form a Yale varsity team.

When Camp presented himself as a candidate,
he was gaining in height and strength, but was not
by any means rugged. His value to the team lay,
apparently, in his speed and his hard-won ability
to kick the ball. Football reputations, like those
won in other pursuits, often come in unexpected
ways. Camp was not pugnacious. But you will
find that his first success came from a rough-and-
tumble fight on the field.

In the Harvard game in 1876, a fully mature
Harvard player, bearded and brawny and strong,
bore down on Walter Camp under the impression
that Camp had the ball. As he was not in possession of it, the tackle should not have been made.
But it was made. And Camp and the Harvard
man engaged, then and there, in a private wrestling
match on the field. They heaved and hauled, and
at last, to everyone's astonishment, Camp threw his
burly opponent and pinned his shoulders down.
Camp was soon thereafter made a member of the
Yale wrestling team.

Recalling Camp at this time, Walter Jennings says that he was "tall, slender, and light; nobody thought he would ever be robust. But he had taken long runs around New Haven in the evening, and he had both speed and stamina. He lacked natural ability for sports, but his real love of them carried him through."

Football was his first love, and all his life it remained his true love among sports. But he played on the Yale baseball team as outfielder, shortstop, and relief pitcher; he appeared on the cinder path in the dashes and hurdles, and was credited with an improvement in the steps taken between the hurdles; he rowed in his class crew, won swimming races at various distances, and represented Yale in the first intercollegiate tennis tournament. A pleasant side of his character is found in the statement of Dr. Samuel W. Lambert that his success in games never made him aloof or proud; he was always ready to play in a scrub game of any kind, or to box or row or wrestle with men who did these things merely for exercise and recreation.

But for six years, through the college and the medical school years, Camp helped to make modern football, and football helped to make him. In his sophomore year, 1877, he first attended an intercollegiate football convention as a delegate from Yale, so beginning the long association with the legislative side of the game, which was to continue with no pause until he died, forty-eight years

later, during the sessions of the Football Rules
Committee in New York.

To give Camp's career as a player, game by
game, would be impossible within the limits of this
book. The game itself has changed so vastly that
the stories of these old games, as the players tell
them, are almost incomprehensible to a boy or
man who plays football now, or watches it. Measured by scores alone, it is interesting to note
that Camp played in five football games against
Harvard, of which Yale won four and tied one.
Camp's field goal won the game in 1880, along
with a touchdown scored by R. W. Watson. But
you cannot measure Camp's ability as a kicker
against that of Brickley, for example, because the
men of those days kicked under such widely different conditions. There was no centre to pass
the ball, no scrimmage of the modern kind; there
were no signals, as we now understand them.
Under modern rules, the kicker may take a pot
shot at the goal with almost as much detachment
as if he were a rifleman aiming at a target. He
may come into the game when called on, and kick
or miss the goal with only the smallest chance of
any physical contact whatever. The men of
Camp's day were expected to play through two
forty-five-minute halves, and on a longer field.
They were obliged to pick up the ball from the
ground, dodge or outrun their opponents, and
often to kick while running at speed. Camp grew

expert at this difficult feat. It is curious that two of the greatest disappointments of his playing career sprang from his perfect performance of it.

In the Harvard game of 1878, played in Boston, Yale stopped a Harvard advance almost on Yale's goal line. Camp and Watson carried the ball, in alternating rushes, to the centre of the field. There Camp broke free for a longer run, and finally evaded the entire Harvard team except one man. As this man bore down on him, Camp still ran at speed until, thirty-five yards away from the touch line, he suddenly checked himself and delivered a drop-kick which shot the ball high over the tackler's head. While the ball was spinning through the air, the whistle blew to end the game. Under the rules then in effect, Camp's magnificent effort went for nothing. The ball flew over the goal posts less than one second too late.

This thirty-five yard kick, executed while making a long run, was matched by Camp in the Harvard game of the following year. Just before the end of the first half, Camp undertook a long kick. The ball rose above the Harvard players who tried to intercept it, sailed straight for the goal, and slid over the posts after a flight of more than forty-five yards. But Bland Ballard of Princeton, referee in this game, had discovered a Yale player holding his opponent. He called back the ball, and Camp's mighty kick had no value. Had it been allowed, it would have won the game — which was the only game tied by Harvard while Camp was in a Yale uniform.

Two more heavy disappointments should be mentioned, for fear it might be thought that Camp was one of those players who do not know the feeling of failure. On the contrary, football's most thorough historian, Parke H. Davis, of Princeton, declares that "no player in the history of the game ever contended against greater misfortunes in his scoring plays than did Walter Camp." One of these "catastrophes," as Mr. Davis calls them, befell Walter Camp in the Princeton game in 1877. The rules were then in embryo, and the methods of scoring were especially in dispute. Columbia, Harvard, and Princeton had agreed that four touchdowns should equal in value one goal from the field. Yale did not agree, and met Princeton on the field after a conference at which it was decided that touchdowns should have no scoring value at all. Yale's players urged this decision and succeeded — unfortunately for themselves — in having it carried. For, not long after the game started, a long and low kick sent the ball squarely into Camp's arms. He caught it, and side-stepped and dodged through the whole Princeton team, running eighty yards for a touchdown. This play, which would now score five points, only gave Yale the right to a free kick at goal. The kick failed.

Camp had another opportunity in the second half of the same game. He secured the ball, this time,

from the old "scrum" formation, and again eluded
all opponents until, after a forty-yard run, he was
almost at the Princeton touch line. It is reported
that McNair, Minor, and Clark of Princeton
tackled him all at once, or nearly so. He fell,
twisted himself free, rose, and plunged over the
line. But again the try for goal was unsuccessful.

Thus in a single game Camp had scored two
touchdowns, after two runs hardly ever equaled in
length and brilliancy by a single player in a game
against good opponents. But his efforts went for
nothing, and the game ended in a tie.

As a player, Camp came through these vicissitudes with his head held high. And later, as chief
strategist for Yale, he met other bitter disappointments in the same sportsmanlike way, accepting
with good grace the referee's decision on plays that
took victory away from Yale. For instance,
there will be described in its proper place a close
decision by William S. Langford that helped Harvard to win its most unexpected victory in recent
years. Camp accepted that decision with true
sportsmanship, even writing to Langford to con-
gratulate him on his work in that game. "You,"
he wrote to the official, "were in a position to see."

Sportsmanship was so much a part of Camp's
character that it remains the thing by which he is
chiefly known. It is for this reason that I have
tried to emphasize the sternly competitive side of
his character — the wish to excel. He was not

among those flabby people who can accept defeat
cheerfully because they have not set their hearts
on victory.

And there was nothing flabby about the games
in which he played. They were primitive, but
hard. The football field on which Camp began
his active career was 140 yards in length and 70
yards wide. The *Harvard Advocate*, in its report of
the Yale–Harvard game in 1876, states unexpectedly that "the two teams presented a very
pretty appearance in their bright new uniforms."
But it goes on to say that "pieces of clothesline
supplied the place of crossbars. There was only a
faint streak of lime to mark the touch lines. Dis-
putes among the players began immediately and
were kept up during the game. The most fla-
grant abuse of the rules was interference when off
side."

There were no pads in the uniforms in those
days, no headgear except knitted caps. In
the Harvard game in 1881 at New Haven, as
Thomas C. Thacher of Harvard remembers it, a
cold and driving rain soon wet the lightly clad
players to the skin. But after the forty-five
minutes of the first half the players lay on the field
or walked around to keep as warm as they could;
there were no dressing-rooms, no chance for rub-
downs or dry clothes. And in all the records of
these games you find the word, "brutality." It
was on this account that the Harvard faculty abol-

ished football at Harvard in 1885, and reinstated it only after long discussions in the following year. Brutality took the form of stand-up fights between the players, and of jumping upon a prostrate opponent in the hope of crippling him. Without the severe and quickly applied penalties for needless roughness which Walter Camp imposed in the course of football legislation during the next two decades, football would by now have become outlawed among sportsmen.

A little of the flavor of the old-time games comes back to us through the mist of the years that lie between. Men ran hard through the two long halves; they accepted bad injuries with almost Indian stoicism, for there were no substitutes and the original players often stayed on the field long after they should have been in the hospital; they mixed it up with their fists, in the absence of rules that prevented such struggles; and they were often torn apart by the referee and their fellow players, only to stay in the game and mix it up again. Through it all you may see the thin and wiry figure of Walter Camp, protecting himself against attacks but not initiating them, and always ready for a long run or a long kick — then, as now, the two great scoring weapons of the game. He could kick, pass, and run. He would have made a "triple-threat" man of the first magnitude in the modern game.

Sportsmanship begets sportsmanship. It flourishes wherever a man consistently displays it. Walter Camp was once asked what incident in his playing career had been the happiest. He did not remember some hard-won victory on the field, or some brilliant play of his own. He said that the brightest moment of all had come in one of the years when he was captain at Yale. The other players seriously objected to his decision that a player who had broken training rules must be dropped from the team.

"They told me," he said, "that this man had learned his lesson, and must be reinstated for the good of the team. I knew that he could not be trusted, and that I had given him every opportunity to deserve confidence. I did not make a hasty decision, and I felt that it must be obeyed. We had a very hot argument, and I resigned the captaincy and left the room. I wanted to play in the coming game, but I did not believe I could give my best efforts in behalf of a team with the members of which I was in such radical disagreement. I spent a very bad night, asking myself if I was doing the right thing, or merely giving way to the spirit of revenge — in which case, I would be both hurting myself and hurting Yale. The happiest moment in my college days came soon afterward, when the men returned and told me that they knew my motives were right, that my decision should stand, and that I was to become their captain again."

Graduating from this hard school of experience, Walter Camp found his college days exceptionally pleasant. The diaries of his classmates are full of pleasant references to him. In one such diary his name occurs on nearly every page. There are glimpses of him playing many games; and we find him sometimes, as a freshman, leaving a party of classmates to walk out and see the varsity baseball team practise, or to undertake some of his own private exercises, like the long, conditioning runs which he had accomplished in school. He played cards assiduously and skillfully, though with little interest in the money side of such games; his allowance was extremely small. But he liked the stretching of wits that is part of a card game. He wrote a great deal of doggerel, and some of it, after practice, became good and flowing verse. He studied hard, but not too hard for companionship. He was elected to a senior society, and was in every way one of the most popular men of his time. His strong interest in anatomy made the choice of medicine and surgery an entirely natural one, although even now, some of his closest friends wonder why he did not go into finance. "He would have made a shrewd and useful dealer in securities," says his closest associate in business, "and he might have created the same reforms in the Stock Exchange that he did in football." But this did not happen. He entered the Yale Medical School, and studied faithfully for two years. Then a very strange thing happened.

Meeting his friend, Walter Jennings, on a summer day in New York, Walter Camp remarked that he had left the Medical School and was looking for a chance in business.

"You are joking," said Jennings. "You can't be serious. Why, you are practically a doctor now. And you will be a wonderfully good doctor. You can't mean to throw it up after all your study."

"But I do," returned Camp.

"Is there any good reason?"

"The fact is," said Walter Camp, "that I can't bear the sight of blood."

If you have any picture of him as a hard or callous man, who was attracted to football by its resemblance to war, by its toughness, this little story will be revealing. We can admit that football is the hardest game that the human mind ever invented. It is bloody enough to-day, and it was bloodier in 1882. Walter Camp had fought his way to success in that game, taking punishment and giving it. He had forced himself to work in the dissection room at the Medical School, to watch operations, and to learn to operate. But the real gentleness of his nature made this work repugnant to him. One can imagine him winning very high honors as a physician or surgeon. He had the charm of manner, the keen love of research, and the exceedingly systematic habits of mind and body which make a great doctor.

His entrance into the Medical School was perhaps the only serious decision in his life which he came afterward to regret. He could not force his spirit to accept what he found there. Having decided that he had made a mistake, he left the school with the knowledge that he had wasted two years of his life. It is true that his medical training helped him a little in his work in later life, but only a little. He might have studied physiology at any time, without taking the other courses required of a medical student.

You will gain a new impression of Camp's gentleness by remembering that he could not bear the sight of blood.

III

THE CALL OF THE FIELD

"He had a patent on football," says Frederick Trevor Hill. "It was Camp's game, and he made up the rules as he went along. Under such conditions, it was almost impossible to beat Yale."

These conditions were not brought about, however, without hard effort on the part of Camp. In the first place, as a young man in business, with no private income, he had no time to give football his full attention during the mornings and afternoons of each day. He had to find — and he did find — someone who could patiently collaborate with him. The discovery of this person was, beyond doubt, the most astonishing good fortune of his whole career.

In the second place, Camp was obliged to dominate the minds of all other football men, most of whom represented other colleges and were naturally anxious to play under rules of their own and to beat Yale.

Camp's success came from the fact that he was observant and logical on the field, and diplomatic in the committee room. He was usually the first of the football legislators to know what should be done. But he was not the first to give his opinion.

He could sit quietly through meetings of any length, until, in despair of reaching an agreement, one of the other men would say : —

"Well, let us see what Walter thinks about it."

At such a moment, Walter Camp was always ready with a clear and logical opinion, which seldom failed of adoption. He judged the trend of the game just as a business man judges the trend of the market. He spoke so confidently, when the time was ripe, that his decisions and suggestions seemed boldly original, simply because other men had not seen with equal penetration the growth of circumstances.

He was no doubt the first American athletic coach who kept a notebook. In fact, he began to keep one while he was still at school, and he never outgrew its use. Watching a football play, or taking part in it himself, he saw the possibilities of improved tactics by noting down the actions of the players, and the way in which they were distributed to meet attack, or grouped and moved to help the carrier of the ball.

All these observations, no matter how inconclusive, were entered in Camp's book. After the games he studied his notes, and with their help devised new ways of advancing the ball and new formations for defense. Thanks to this systematic observation, no thoughts were forgotten and no inspiration escaped him. He was not particularly inventive. He could depend on no sudden inspiration. But if he was not boldly original, he was at least methodically sure. He amassed more information than any other player or coach, and he studied his notes from one end of the year to the other, wringing from them the sound ideas which made him eminent as football player, coach, and legislator.

"I try," he said, "to keep one jump ahead."

There is an interesting proof of his ability to keep a little ahead of an opponent in the story of a Yale–Princeton baseball game played in 1880 at New York. Camp was a good batter, with a sure eye and a well-controlled swing. But he was not famous as a maker of long hits. It surprised everyone when he made a home run off the first ball pitched to him.

Coming to bat again, Camp rightly decided that the Princeton pitcher would not expect him to swing hard at the first ball. Lightning is supposed not to strike twice in the same place. But Camp did swing hard at the first ball, and made a second home run.

Later in the game, he faced the pitcher for the third time. There was an interesting, if silent, battle of wits between the two men. Camp rightly thought that the pitcher would like to waste the first ball, by pitching it so far from the plate that Camp could not touch it. But that would show fear of the batter. It might unsettle the other Princeton men. It was reasonable to suppose that the pitcher would make a desperate effort to pitch a strike, over the plate. The pitcher's mind worked exactly as Camp thought it would. The first ball came over the plate. Camp swung at it with confidence, and knocked out a third home run.

This record is probably unique in baseball records: three pitched balls, three home runs. Camp had outguessed the pitcher, and had maintained himself one jump ahead. He had made his natural skill doubly strong by supporting it with his unsleeping mind. In his fourteen baseball games against Harvard, he made seventeen hits. This is not a great batting record, nor did Camp regard himself as more than a fair batsman. Of these fourteen games, seven were won by each side. The season of 1880 was the most successful of them. In that year Camp, in left field, formed with Wilbur Parker at third base, George Clark at right field, and William F. Hutchinson at short-stop, a quartette which has seldom been surpassed in college baseball. Hutchinson, as some of his classmates recall, would have been Yale's regular pitcher if there had been a catcher capable of holding him. But he pitched in batting practice, and Parker said later: "After the pitching Hutchinson gave us in practice, whatever the other pitchers could offer looked like balloons." But Yale had great pitchers before then; for instance, on May 26, 1877, C. F. Carter pitched for Yale and dismissed Harvard without either a hit or a run.

Such details will convince young readers that baseball has changed much less than football. Mann of Princeton and Avery of Yale were pitching curve balls as early as 1875. Catcher's mitts were used a year or two later, and F. W. Thayer of Harvard invented the catcher's mask in 1877. Baseball uniforms were similar to those worn now, and the general strategy of the game was the same. Football has changed much more. Only the halfbacks and fullbacks retain the same name, and their duties are very different. The field is shorter and narrower, and is marked out with lines that are responsible for the name, "grid-iron." Camp never heard that name in his college days, though he was to invent the type of game that made it necessary. These changes in football will be discussed in their proper order. Meanwhile, remember that baseball has changed very little in spirit, and football has changed much. The direction of baseball is in professional hands. It was certain, even in Camp's college days, that the public would support professional baseball. It is not certain, even now, that professional football will win such support. Football is still basically an amateur game, played in a sportsmanlike spirit. If there seems to you to be more chivalry in football than in baseball, you may correctly ascribe it to the influence of Walter Camp.

Take, for instance, the one detail of squabbling with the officials. It is very much alive in professional baseball; it may come to life in professional football, but it is no part of amateur football. A story of Camp's own early career will help to give the reason.

In the season of 1885, Walter Camp was chosen by Princeton to be the referee in the Yale–Princeton game. It was an extraordinary honor for Camp, a Yale graduate, an intense Yale sympathizer, and the chief adviser of the Yale football team. But the hope of Princeton for a victory was safe in his hands. Princeton's team was a powerful one, and its most powerful player was H. C. Lamar.

During the season, Lamar made consistent long runs against Princeton's opponents. F. T. Hill, visiting Princeton at the request of the Yale coach, reported that these runs always took place from a certain formation, and that, in a manner of speaking, they could be stopped before they started. This information was well used in Yale's preparation for the game. Lamar *was* stopped. And before the game was very old H. Beecher, the Yale quarterback, caught a punt, close to the side of the field. He set off at full speed toward Princeton's goal, slipped like an eel through the fingers of the whole opposing team, and apparently scored a touchdown. But Camp called him back. He ruled that Beecher had stepped out of bounds at the start of his magnificent run, and that the ball was down at that point.

Later, by extraordinary irony, Camp had to make a similarly close decision. All through the game, the great Princeton back had been held to a standstill. It had been a dismal afternoon for him. And, with the last moments of the game slipping away, Yale had the ball, and the chance of a Princeton victory seemed impossible. But then Yale punted down the field — and *not* to Lamar. It was a superb kick by G. A. Watkinson, long and high and well placed. The Princeton quarterback got under it, raising his arms for the catch. The ball struck him on the chest, rebounded, and flew across the field into Lamar's hands. He seized it, and was off down the side line like a flash. One of the greatest football runners who ever lived, he had his chance now. The Yale forwards streamed toward him, too late. W. T. Bull of the Yale backfield and Watkinson raced toward the side line, hoping to tackle Lamar or to force him out of bounds. With the white side line perilously close to his feet as he sped forward, Lamar dashed past Walter Camp, the referee.

"In that instant," said Walter Camp whimsically to Hill, "I exercised the hardest bit of self-control in my life. Lamar thundered by within a yard of me. If I had stuck out my foot —"

He did not stick out his foot. He turned, and

ran with Lamar toward the Yale goal. A few
yards farther along, Lamar had to twist and turn
to dodge Watkinson and Bull. Then he was over
the line, and touching down the ball, after a desperate race nearly the whole length of the field,
and only a stride or two ahead of F. G. Peters, captain of Yale.

Instantly a protest was made. It was thought
that Lamar, like Beecher in the earlier play, had
stepped out of bounds. Camp ruled that he had
not. It was a touchdown. A less honest, less
scrupulous man would have remembered that he
had deprived Yale of one touchdown and would
now seek to balance it by depriving Princeton of
another. But Camp stood fast. Reaching his
judgment with absolute honesty, he was nevertheless so full of desire to see Yale win the game that
he had recognized his urge to trip or tackle Lamar.
The urge was human enough. But in all matters
of honesty and of sportsmanship, Camp was more
than merely human. He allowed Lamar's long
run to stand; and the touchdown which came as a
result of it won the game for Princeton.

It was no wonder that, in the following year,
Harvard's captain, W. A. Brooks, asked Camp to
referee the Yale–Harvard game. Sportsmanship
appeals to sportsmen, and Harvard knew that
there would be absolute fairness at the hands of
Walter Camp. That game, incidentally, resulted
in a comfortable victory for Yale by 29–4, with

two touchdowns by Beecher and five goals kicked by Watkinson helping to take away the sting of defeat by Princeton in the year before.

Camp was not, however, in favor of allowing any college graduate to act as an official in a game in which his own college was concerned. This practice has long ago disappeared. But it is fair to say that, while it endured, Camp did more than any man to prove that a true sportsman cannot be challenged, even while he is serving as umpire or referee. Baseball umpires are often called "robbers." Football officials never are.

You can draw your own opinion of the value to Yale of having a sportsman of Camp's quality on Yale Field during football practice. Camp himself had little idea of his own value in this respect. He knew he was an able coach, but he did not realize fully that he was a Chevalier Bayard — a man almost unrivaled in purity of motive. He could not teach dirty football. He was an example of clean, fair play. I am excluding from this book many of the paragraphs which Camp wrote about the beneficial effects on the character of football training. He measured other men by himself, and did not see how they fell short. Many a coach has taught young football players to slug and to hold, to resort to any kind of dirty trick when there was little chance of detection. Camp knew that these things were taught, but he did not know how often they were taught. His praise of football is sometimes too high, for this reason alone. It can be, and usually is nowadays, a fair, clean fight; but it is not right to suppose that every boy who has played it has been morally benefited as a result.

Although he made his début as a football legislator in his second year at college, it is of Camp as a football coach that one should speak first. It is the queerest part of his whole career, measured by ordinary standards. There are no other coaches like Camp. His work was done, nearly all of it, in the small parlor of his house on Gill Street. He was in active business, and had but little time for coaching on the field. The visible and audible part of his coaching was done after dark, and in his home. Of course, there were few hours in the year when Camp was not *thinking* about football. But he taught it at his own fireside. He was working hard to support his family. His free hours were not in the early afternoons, when football practice is on. He could not go regularly to Yale Field. He needed another pair of eyes, as sharp as his own; another keen, retentive memory upon which the events of each day's practice could be stamped photographically for him to consider in the evenings; and another real set of football brains, against which his own intelligence might rub.

He found all these qualities in his wife.

I am aware, as I write, that it is almost impos-

sible for anyone who did not know Mr. and Mrs.
Camp to believe these words; but you will confirm
the truth by talking with men who went to the
modest house on Gill Street, and heard Mrs. Camp
report the day's doings at Yale Field to her husband and discuss them with him so clearly that he
could understand and use them.   There are in any
profession few such partnerships between husband
and wife.   As a young girl, moreover, Mrs. Camp
had not been interested in athletics.   She was
born into a keenly intellectual family.   William
Graham Sumner, who became one of the greatest
professors ever associated with Yale or any other
university, was her brother.   It was possible for
Professor Sumner, in his lectures on sociology, to
carry his undergraduates far out of the ordinary
world of the classroom, and give them a sudden,
breath-taking vision of the origins and of the
future of mankind.   Alice Graham Sumner may
not have dreamed, in girlhood, that her own intellectual interests were not to be literary or humani-
tarian.   She was a potential novelist or sociologist.
Marrying Walter Camp, she made his interests
her interests.   Intellectually his equal, she became
his helpmate in even the chosen sphere of his own
activities.

The Camp family approached that ideal rela-
tionship where husband and wife are one.
Without Mrs. Camp's help, Walter Camp would
have had no career as football coach and rule-

maker. He would have gone to the games, like any ordinary alumnus, but he would have known no more about football itself than do the casual spectators. Through the devoted coöperation of Mrs. Camp, he was able to become a successful business man and a football authority too. His first interest was the support of his family. Thanks to his wife, he could go to his office every afternoon, and still know exactly what was happening on Yale Field.

He was always, by force of circumstances, more a coach of Yale's coaches than of Yale's players. But the players themselves, the very best of them, came to the little house on Gill Street. Heffelfinger was often there, and the furniture would be pushed back to let him learn, or demonstrate, some new idea in a linesman's play. Year after year the faces of these visitors changed, and it is not necessary to name them here. One of the most teachable — and he has since proved himself an excellent teacher — was T. A. D. Jones.

"Camp coached through the coaches," remarked Jones. "In my time as a player, he seldom took an active part on the field. He came and watched, and when he thought that an end, for instance, could play better by changing his style, Camp would go to the coach of the ends and suggest how the improvement could be made. He had no more authoritative position than treasurer of the Yale Athletic Association, but his advice had authority because it was good advice. The practice then was to have the former year's captain return as head coach. Other old players came up to coach, and Camp, by serving every year as adviser, gave unity and continuity to these shifting assistants. Between the halves, Camp would suggest to the head coach or captain what he had noticed in the first period and give advice on meeting the situation. Exhortations of the style commonly given in locker rooms were not his way. He spoke quietly to individual players, but did not make orations before or during or after a game."

The extraordinary effectiveness of this habit of speaking quietly to individuals is well illustrated in a story told by C. J. La Roche, who was a more or less obscure candidate for quarterback, a year or two before the war. Camp was no longer chief strategist for Yale, but he came to the field occasionally. La Roche made a long run in one of the early games, and repeated it in practice one afternoon.

"Immediately," he said, "I became aware of the two most luminous and gleaming eyes I have ever seen in a man's face. I was almost paralyzed when I realized that Walter Camp was looking at me and speaking to me. It was like being addressed by a god. He showed me a certain way to shift my weight, while running, that he felt would be useful to me. I was dazed by the look in his eyes, but I had just sense enough to remember what he had shown me, and to profit by it."

It was by such methods, although he probably never knew that he startled the young players so much, that Camp was able to teach the things that he knew. La Roche went on to have a thoroughly satisfactory season. Of all the hours and hours of intensive coaching which he received, he remembers best that little minute with Walter Camp.

The home life of the Camps was necessarily very simple. Dollars were few. Camp had chosen a business — the manufacture of clocks — in which the demand is fairly stable, but the profits are not large, nor is there much opportunity for speculation. He used to advise young men to manufacture staple articles, which are never entirely unwanted, even during hard times. His business progress was slow. The New Haven Clock Company was a very old concern, in which young men started at the bottom and often stayed there. Camp saw that his own promotions would not be rapid. He felt satisfied if his income increased regularly a few hundred dollars a year during these early seasons of his business life.

For the call of the field was in his ears. He found that he made friends most easily with people who were genuinely interested in sport. Mr. and Mrs. Lorin F. Deland were ideal friends for the Camps, although they were not Yale football sympathizers at all. In fact, as head coach at

Harvard, Deland's chief purpose was to score victories over Yale teams. It seemed strange to people blinded by partisanship that, in private life, he and Camp were warm friends. But Deland was a graceful essayist, and the father of all modern advertising that has some literary value. Camp had been class poet at Yale, and was trying his hand at novels and other books. Margaret Deland was to become the beloved author of *Old Chester Tales* and *Dr. Lavendar's People*. Mrs. Camp had her own strong intellectual heritage. A common love of football brought Camp and Deland together as irresistibly as iron is drawn to a magnet. Their literary tastes cemented their union still more firmly. In one year, when Yale and Harvard had abandoned their annual game after much mutual recrimination, Camp and Deland improved the occasion by sitting down together to write the first complete book on football. From an intensely partisan standpoint, they should have been glowering at each other from New Haven and Boston, respectively. But they were both sportsmen, and both men of the world. They knew that the breach would be healed, and Yale and Harvard would renew their old rivalry. The book called *Football* came out in 1896 over their joint signatures. It contains much good writing, and much good football too. The army of readers of Mrs. Deland's novels, so far removed in spirit and feeling from football, would be astonished to learn that she drew the fifty-one pictures for it; but they remain, to this day, as proof that she contributed her bit to the improvement of football.

Although Camp and Deland were such successful collaborators, they were keen rivals too. Camp took infinite pleasure in foiling Deland's original plays. Deland would have been equally delighted if he had ever succeeded in piercing Camp's defensive tactics. He was very near it when he invented the famous flying wedge. This peculiar, human battering ram was expected to drive through the Yale defense like a fifteen-inch shell through a wooden fence. It was tried for the first time, after careful preparation in secret, at the Yale–Harvard game in 1892. It was not an unqualified success. The fact is clear, however, that the wedge rammed forward, the first time it was tried, from the centre of the field to Yale's 25-yard line. And it became the father of a whole flock of so-called "momentum plays," which lasted for many years and were only defeated in the long run by legislation against them. Deland was a bolder innovator than Camp, but Camp's teams beat Deland's teams, and the Harvard man was not a person to sit and suffer without making inquiries. He even asked a former Yale football captain to explain Camp's methods.

"Well," said this man, "when we want to know how the Yale team is doing at any time, we don't go to the newspapers to find out. It makes little difference to us what the players are doing; we want to know what the coaches are doing. If they are going up to Walter's every night, then we know that the team is going to be a good one."

But there were times when Camp could come down on the field like a thunderbolt. There were times when he forgot his rôle of keeping behind the scenes, and went into action in a way that permanently influenced the man on whom his displeasure fell. He had a grim streak in his make-up, and a vein of biting humor. He kept it under. But sometimes it broke through his surface calm.

One afternoon a huge freshman, with a pair of enormous shoulders, big hands, and a chin to match, reported for practice with the Yale squad. He tackled in deadly fashion, and smashed interference in a way that left it smashed. But the varsity quarterback soon found, in a practice game, that by sending his runner farther out to the side the ball could be carried easily around the freshman recruit at end. For some time, Walter Camp watched this man charging blindly into the scrimmage where the scrimmage was thickest.

"That won't do," he said to him, after the game ended. "The business of a football end is like that of the troops on the wing of an army. He must not be outflanked. As long as the runner can get between you and the side line, you are worthless to your team."

The big man only grunted, disdaining the advice. And on the following days he made the same mistake, until the field coaches regarded him as unteachable.

Camp finally told some workmen to move a few timbers to the side line. Then he took the big freshman to see the work.

"You know how dogs are often exercised at kennels," he said, quietly. "I want to help you make the team, so I have borrowed the idea. A wire will be run along the top of these posts. Then this chain will be shackled to your belt, and will slide along the wire so that you can run up and down the field just six feet from the side line. Then the runner can't get around you."

The player lost all his surliness. He saw the workmen rigging the wire. He looked into Camp's steady dark eye.

"Take that thing down," he gulped. "I get the idea."

He got the idea so well that no gains were ever again made around his end, during the four years he played for Yale.

IV

HOW FOOTBALL GREW

Boys of to-day are often eager to know about old-time football. They ask, "What was it like?" There is no better answer than is given by Parke H. Davis in his "Fifty Years of Intercollegiate Football," which I quote by permission from the 1926 edition of Spalding's *Official Football Guide*.

"The first man in the line was called the 'end rush,'" writes Mr. Davis. "The second man was at first designated as the 'next to end,' the third as the 'next to centre,' and the fourth, of course, as the 'centre.' It quickly was noticed that the 'next to end' made more tackles than any other man, and so he came to be known as the 'tackler,' a name later changed to 'tackle.' Similarly, it was noticed that the 'next to centre' guarded the 'centre' by bracing him, so he came to be called the 'guard.' . . . In the old Rugby 'scrum' neither side had possession of the ball; it came haphazard out of scrimmage to whichever side could capture it. Another feature of the early game, which is remembered with humor, was the system of officials. These consisted of an umpire for each side, with a referee to decide disagreements between the umpires. The two umpires discharged their duties like an opposing pair of football lawyers. In fact, they frequently were chosen more for their argumentative abilities than for their knowledge of the game.

"The tactics of the times made the play essentially a kicking game. The backs kicked punts, drop kicks, and place kicks. Even the 'rushers,' or forwards, also kicked the ball when opportunity arose. Not only was the ball kicked as at present, but it was kicked, and cleverly kicked, while bouncing upon the ground. An accurate drop-kicker to-day is a valuable possession for any eleven, but where in recent years has appeared such a spectacular performer as Alexander Moffatt of Princeton, who kicked thirty-two field goals in fifteen games, having kicked no less than six drops against Pennsylvania in 1883?

"The game was opened, as now, by a kick-off. The player of 1880 might, if he chose, drive the ball far down the field. Or, technically kicking the ball by merely touching it with his toe, he might pick it up and run with it. Players when tackled invariably endeavored to pass the ball back to another member of their side for a further advance, a method of play so highly developed that it was not infrequent to see a ball passed as many as five times during a single play."

Supplementing Mr. Davis's remarks, it may be permissible to add that football is still played in much the same way in England, and that English players regard our American game as inferior to theirs in pleasure for the participants. But soccer is an infinitely more popular game abroad than Rugby football. Rugby football lacks decisiveness. A team does not profit sufficiently, as a team, by ability to hold on to the ball and follow one advance with another. Rugby football is full of kaleidoscopic action, but it has not the driving force or the sustained dramatic action of American football. In this chapter we shall see how our game was made, and why Walter Camp may properly be called its father.

Camp's first appearance at a football convention was in his junior year at Yale. He startled the meeting of the delegates at the Massasoit House, in Springfield, on October 9, 1878, by recommending that the number of players be reduced from fifteen to eleven. This resolution was defeated. Camp presented it again in the following year, and again it failed. In that year he also proposed that "safeties" — the plays in which the ball is carried by a team behind its own goal line — be declared scoring plays and be given a value adverse to the team which made them. This plan was also, for the time being, rejected by the delegates. But in the year that followed, Camp studied the game and waited. The convention in Springfield, on October 12, 1880, brought a threefold victory for Camp.

It was his contention that the old-fashioned scrum was nothing but a scramble. The ball was set down on the field, and both teams clustered around it, with all the rushers kicking at the ball and trying to drive it free from the forest of legs all around it. This seemed to Camp an absurd and disorderly way to start play. Neither side could practise strategy, because neither knew when, or at what point, the ball would come out of the scrum. This uncertainty was only slightly removed by a crude form of tactics in which certain players became skilled in squeezing the ball under their feet to make it leap out in a desired direction. But this was difficult and unreliable. Camp declared that the game needed sharp revision ; that it should be a game of brains, not of chance. He maintained that neither the players nor the public would be interested in the game unless it became orderly. Football, to his mind, was not alone a clash of bodies, nor a running race. It needed finesse, generalship, consistent and continued strategy. These were not possible from such a scramble as the scrum formation.

If a well-planned attack were to be possible, and the finer elements of the tactics were to come into the game, Camp declared that it was necessary to give one side undisputed possession of the ball, with leave to hold it as long as systematic advances were made. Only the failure to make consistent gains ought to defeat a team. Simple luck should not be allowed to upset an otherwise able offensive. Camp pressed this point. It had weight. The delegates understood that, if it were not accepted, football would not become a popular sport. Camp had sufficient prestige, by this year, to demand fair play and a fair chance for all. He broke new ground with the invention of the scrimmage. He planned to give possession of the ball to one side, permitting this team to put it into play without interference by opponents. This still remains the greatest single difference between Rugby football and American football, and it was Walter Camp's invention.

At the football convention in 1880 were W. H. Manning and T. C. Thacher, representing Harvard; E. S. Peace and Francis Loney for Princeton; Robert W. Watson and W. B. Hill for Yale. Before proposing the scrimmage, Camp presented his twice rejected resolution to reduce the number of players to eleven on each team. This time it was carried. Then Camp presented the following rule, which he had prepared: —

A scrimmage takes place when the holder of the ball puts it on the ground before him, and puts it into play either by kicking the ball, or by snapping it back with his foot.

Some years were to pass before, by gradual evolution, the present method of putting the ball into play with the hands was arrived at. At first the snapper-back used his foot. Later he placed one hand on the ball to guide it.

This scrimmage proposal caused a lively debate, but it was accepted without a dissenting vote. It was frankly a step into the dark. No one among the delegates could know, nor could Camp tell them, what the consequence might be.

As part of the same rule establishing the scrimmage, Camp invented the position of quarterback, by prescribing that "the man who first receives the ball from the snap-back shall be called the quarterback, and shall not rush forward with the ball under penalty of foul."

Modern football, with its consistent strategy, began at the conference in 1880. All that has come since is a logical development. The teams were reduced to eleven men, the scrimmage was provided for, and the key position on the team, the quarterback, was established. The signals now called by the quarterback, the different way in which the ball is passed to the runners, the variations of team offense and defense, are all natural outgrowths of Camp's innovations. While still an undergraduate at Yale, he had originated the eleven, the scrimmage, and the quarterback — three inventions which of themselves alone would have won him a place in football's Hall of Fame. But he did not stop. He applied himself, as did every other coach and captain, to find out what could be done under the new rules he had framed.

Each captain went back from that conference with an entirely new set of problems. How were the eleven men to be arranged? Harvard lined up with seven rushers, one fullback, and three halfbacks, who took turns acting as quarterback. Princeton appeared on the field with six players on the line, one quarterback, two fullbacks, and two halfbacks. Walter Camp deployed the Yale team with seven men on the line, and four in the backfield; one quarterback, two halfbacks, and one fullback. This proved the best formation, and became standard. Camp's competitive genius here asserted itself against the competition of other strategists. His formation proved itself the most flexible of the three, allowing a greater variety of plays to be run. It was logical, when the quarterback had been invented, for that player to become the field general of the team. The ball came to him first from the centre. The use of signals to inform the team what play was to be used — without at the same time informing the adversaries — was also a logical development, which Walter Camp was first to recognize and first to use. The code of signals given to Yale was ludicrously simple, providing for only four plays. The signals were not numerals, as at present, but short sentences. Each entire sentence indicated a play, the omission of one word, and then another, serving to hide the meaning. Thus, the sentence, "Look out quick, Deac," or any word from it, meant in Camp's code: "Twombley will start the next play to the right, ball being passed to Peters." And the sentence, "Play up sharp, Charley," or any part of it, would indicate that the ball would be passed through quarterback to W. Terry for a run to the left. These were simple signals, but perhaps just as effective as the intricate mathematical symbols used nowadays, sometimes misunderstood in the moment of greatest need by a weary team.

But Camp's one outstanding invention was the scrimmage. Some of his friends regard it as the greatest single invention that has been made in any game during the memory of man. For Camp practically invented American football when he invented it. The number of players does not matter very much. The size of the field and the distance to be gained in three downs or four downs, is a detail. But the scrimmage is the cardinal, essential feature of the game.

Oddly enough, it had immediate results which were as unexpected as they were absurd. In fact they threatened to make football so dull that nobody could bear to look at it, much less to play it. It will be noticed that the scrimmage rule, as quoted above, gives the ball into undisputed possession of one side. But it does not take the ball away from that side. Unless a fumble or a kick occurs, the side which has the ball, under this rule, can hang on to it forever. Camp had assumed, when he framed the rule, that the old practice of constant punting would continue, and that the ball would therefore change hands very often.

But E. S. Peace of Princeton, who had helped to put the rule into effect, and his colleague, P. T. Bryan, another Princeton strategist, studied the rule and found the flaw in it. Carefully and systematically they developed, behind closed gates, Princeton's attack against Yale. But when the game was played they discovered that Walter Camp had drilled Yale in a similar attack just like their own.

From any sporting standpoint, that game was unutterably silly. Princeton's turn came first. Winning the toss, the Princeton team took the ball and never relinquished it throughout the first half. The game was dreary before it was ten minutes old. Play after play failed to gain, but still Princeton held the ball. Fourth down was followed by fourteenth down and fortieth down — although, of course, downs were not counted under those rules. At last the intermission came. It was hoped that Yale might brighten up the play during the second half. But Walter Camp started the half by dribbling the ball and then running with it. Yale's ball. It was still Yale's ball, on practically the same spot, when the half ended, forty-five minutes later.

If it had been Walter Camp's purpose in inventing the scrimmage to permit continuous strategy, he must have been startled by this result. Princeton had the entire first half in which to develop her strategy, and the Yale team enjoyed the same unbroken opportunity throughout the second half.

But from the grandstands the game was ridiculous, and it was no better for the men on the field, after heaving and hauling for a whole afternoon with such a deplorable lack of results. There was a clamor in the newspapers. Yale was still technically champion of the association, because under the rules, in event of a tie, the championship rested with the previous year's winner. But Walter Camp came forward quickly for Yale, with the following rule, presented to the football convention at its next session : —

If on three consecutive fairs and downs a team shall not have advanced the ball five yards, nor lost ten, they must give up the ball to the opponents at the spot of the fourth down.

This rule required the five-yard line marks on the playing field, from which came the name of "gridiron," now so familiar. And from this rule, too, came the phrase "yards to gain," another contribution to the phraseology of the game.

In practice, however, even this requirement was found to be an insufficient improvement. Teams, rather than lose possession of the ball when their advance was halted, resorted to deliberate tactical retreats, and by retiring ten yards gained a new opportunity to re-launch their attack. In this way a kick, with its surrender of the ball, could be avoided for a long time. The result was not much different from the earlier "block game" which the regulation had been designed to prevent, and football again was threatened with disfavor. More important, however, from Camp's point of view, was the unfairness of the strategy. It enabled a weaker team to hold the ball by deliberate retreats, and so to deny its opponents their rightful chance to prove their superior worth. Camp hated unfairness. He warred against the possibility that an able opponent might be deprived of well-earned victory through anything except the clearly-demonstrated strength of its rivals. He did not want the football rules to become a refuge for weaklings. He dreaded inconclusive games, because he knew that the fun of a contest lies in the fun of a victory.

In legislating, remember that what a gentleman wants is fair play and the best man to win [he wrote]. When it is possible without losing sight of this, to legislate for improvements in methods, so much the better; but primarily make every rule such that the probability of unfinished, drawn, or disputed contests is reduced to a minimum.

Thereupon, when the so-called "five-or-ten-yard rule" had been shown to be inadequate, he helped to give it new effectiveness by increasing the length of an enforced retreat to twenty yards. The advantage of strategic retirements was thus eliminated, more frequent punts were necessary, and the game was automatically made more "open," to the increased advantage of players and spectators alike.

But the open character of play was later to be lost, inadvertently and through a change in rules which had been thought slight, but which had a momentous effect. For several years the team on the offensive had usually been placed in a far-flung line across the playing field, and the ball was tossed laterally by the quarterback to put the play in motion. This was the "open" game so much enjoyed at the time, and so vociferously regretted when, by mischance, it was sacrificed. Apparently, Walter Camp again led in upsetting the "open" tactics. It was done by a very simple suggestion, which seemed comparatively unimportant. A proposal was made, at a football rules convention, that the form of tackling be changed, to permit a tackle to be made as low as the knees. The proposal was adopted. Until then, the Rugby form of tackling, at the shoulders or the waist, had been used.

But now the tackles acquired a new effectiveness. It was found that a runner, tackled at the knees, was instantly stopped. He could seldom be pulled or pushed for additional gain. He was thrown in his tracks. The defense was immeasurably strengthened. A runner in the open field was faced with new difficulties in trying to advance with the ball, for he could no longer struggle forward after being tackled by a defensive opponent.

This shifted the entire character of the play, and made open-field running less attractive than it had been. The profit was taken away from it, and the greater chance of gaining ground was found to be in weight-plays. Because a single runner could be effectively stopped, coaches developed mass formations protecting the runners, and driving them forward by the sheer momentum of team-mates pulling and pushing them on. The players on the attacking team, accordingly, were drawn in close together, shoulder to shoulder, and there began the mass plays, the heaps of players, the close, confusing tactics which remained an unattractive character of football until the 1905 upheaval forced a change. The cause of this extraordinary consequence had seemed unimportant — simply that tackles might be made as low as the knees; but it resulted in the game's most critical phase.

For, as football grew, it attracted an enormous amount of public attention, not always of a favorable sort. It passed through periods when its very existence was threatened. The two greatest storms were in the early 90's, and in 1904–05. For the first storm Walter Camp had himself been largely responsible. But he was used to bearing criticism. Ten years before, he had been involved in sharp discussions of the eligibility rules. He believed that football should be strictly an amateur sport. By its own rough nature, he felt, it was more vulnerable to abuse through loosely observed

standards than any other major sport. Camp
determined to purge football of professionalism by
limiting the eligibility of all players in the association. He had made a start at this while he was
still a graduate student at Yale. Having been
elected captain of the Yale baseball team while
he was in the Medical School, Camp declined to
accept the honor, on the ground that college teams
should be led by undergraduates. Subsequently
he broadened his views, and became an ardent
supporter of a rule limiting intercollegiate athletics
to undergraduate students.

This purpose brought him into sharp conflict
with the representatives of the other colleges in
the football association which had been founded at
the first Springfield convention, and which was the
parent of the present Football Rules Committee.
In 1882, at a convention in Springfield, a rule was
adopted that "no man shall be allowed in championship games for a longer period than five years."
Camp had ended his own playing days in the preceding year, and had represented Yale for six
years. But the new regulation found a warm
champion in him.

Slowly at first, and then with great impetus, a
situation was developing that made this ideal im-
perative. By 1889 the presence of graduate players
on the teams became such an open abuse that the
newspapers took notice. In that year, as Parke
H. Davis has noted in his football histories, the

prospects of the Princeton and Harvard teams
were especially discouraging. Many valuable
players had graduated from both these colleges,
and it seemed that the teams must be composed
of inexperienced players. But suddenly the situation altered. Two veteran football players became graduate students at Princeton, and two
others matriculated there for special studies. At
Harvard two experienced football men enrolled for
graduate work, and another became a special student. At Yale, likewise, four veterans reported
for football practice as members of the graduate
schools. Games had already become worth winning. The teams were worth strengthening. The
"galaxy of graduates," as Mr. Davis calls it, was
a proof of the growing importance of the sport.
To add more power to the critics who began at once
to complain about the debasement of the sport,
there were plentiful rumors that the amateur
standing of many players was not what it should
be, and that many graduate players had been induced by something more lucrative than a graduate
degree to pursue their higher education.

At this juncture, Yale and Wesleyan — where
Woodrow Wilson was interested in the football
coaching — called for a special meeting to consider
"certain questions of amateur standing." This
movement, largely sponsored by Camp and Wilson,
was strongly supported by the newspapers, and by
public opinion as well. The game was in great

danger of becoming corrupt. Politics played
an important part in the discussions which followed.

In November 1889 the special convention assembled at the Fifth Avenue Hotel in New York
City. Harvard was represented there by H. C.
Leeds of the class of 1877; Pennsylvania's delegate was John C. Bell, '84; Duncan Edwards, '85,
and E. A. Poe, '91, spoke for Princeton; F. D.
Beattys, '85, was Wesleyan's representative; and
Walter Camp, '80, appeared in Yale's behalf.
Camp almost immediately offered a resolution
declaring that "no one shall be eligible to take
part as a player in any championship games of
this association who is not a bona-fide student of
the college on whose team he plays, matriculated
for the then current year, and regularly pursuing
a course which requires his attendance upon at
least five lectures or recitations a week," and stipu-
lating further that "no professional athlete shall
take part in any contest of this association, nor
shall any player of any university or college be
paid or receive, directly or indirectly, any money
or financial concession or emolument as present or
past compensation for, or as a prior consideration
or inducement to, playing, whether the same be
received from or paid by or at the instance of the
football association, athletic committee, or faculty of
such college or university, or any individual whatsoever." The resolution, as Camp presented it,

provided also an elaborate system for challenging players whose eligibility was doubted, and for allowing these players to meet such challenges.

Despite its formal language, it is well to read Camp's resolution carefully. There is no doubt that it would have put football on a simon-pure amateur basis. The old attack had been on graduate players — husky, bearded men, who had the tremendous advantage of being allowed to oppose mere boys. But Camp was now shifting the attack. Notice the words "or any individual whatsoever." This is a thrust at the disguised form of professionalism which exists whenever a college graduate, wishing for football victory, quietly pays the tuition fee or living expenses or both — either in whole or in part — of some former schoolboy star, who agrees in return to go to the college specified and try for its football team. Many a man, reaching into his pocket for this purpose, has felt that he was benefiting both the boy and the college football team. Many a graduate, old enough to know better, has seduced an immature boy by promising him either money or its equivalent in receipted bills. And if the resolution offered by Camp is ancient history, the abuse against which it was directed is still very much alive. Writing in the May 27, 1926, issue of *The Youth's Companion*, B. Friedman, quarterback in 1925 of the University of Michigan team, makes this specific comment: —

The high school boy who succeeds in athletics is given, as he nears the end of his school career, the grand athletic rush.   He is the object of attention by college graduates, field secretaries, and the scouts of college alumni associations.   He is interviewed by men of engaging manners, some of them super-salesmen.

I will relate what happened to my high school chum and myself.   We had both done fairly well in school sports during our senior year.   We were visited by men representing colleges.   We attended banquets and theatre parties all arranged for us by these men.   We were in a daze.   I changed my mind at least twice a week.   At last a certain college seemed to be the real choice.   This college was not offering me anything for my football ability !   I was to have a scholarship based on the grades I would get.   If I received all A's, then I would be paid $300, and the sum varied according to the grades.   I was also promised a job.   But I finally decided to go to Michigan, which was nearer home. Michigan offered me no scholarship, and did not even promise me a job.   I enrolled at Michigan, and secured two jobs, working in a bookstore when not attending classes in the daytime, and working in the evening at a motion picture theatre. . . .   It was a hard grind, and I once became so discouraged that I had my grip packed and was on the way to the railroad station, when it dawned on me that I was being a quitter of the rankest kind.   I turned about, went back to my room, and returned to my studies.

During the vacation period I was lucky enough to get a good job.   I saved up enough money so that in my sophomore year I could afford to give up the theatre job.   I had more opportunity for study and got a great deal more sleep.   I have been supremely well satisfied. I found the university and the kind of studies I wanted. I was fortunate in football.   Since I earned every cent of what my stay in Michigan cost me, and the money came in such a difficult way, I have studied all the harder to get a full return on my investment, and I have been much happier.

My chum was not better fixed financially than I was. An Eastern college made him a flattering offer.   He would not have to do any outside work to earn his money.   All he had to do was walk to the athletic office once every month and draw his check.   All he had to do in return was to play football.   He accepted the offer.   At the end of his first semester, it was discovered that he lacked the required credits.   He and I had been prepared in an academic high school, and this was a technical college that he found himself enrolled in.   He could not continue in athletics, and for that matter, he could not continue in college.   A wealthy alumnus came to his rescue, sending him to a preparatory school and paying all his expenses.   When the tutors had finished their work, he was fitted to resume his college duties.   By this time he realized his grave mistake.   He talked it over with me during vacation time, and we tried to think of some scheme by which he could honorably discharge his obligations to the college and leave.   He has a keen sense of honor and duty.   He decided that he was bound to see it through.   He had taken checks from the college, and he owed it his services on the gridiron.   The fact that he owed these services made football playing a hard task to him, and one that he abhorred. His heart has never been in the work, and he — who should have developed into one of the greatest of football stars — will never come anywhere near the niche he is capable of filling. How can he, under the circumstances?

When a boy is paid to play college football, neither party to the contract gets much out of it. The boy will never play his best, so he makes himself a poor investment, and he can get no worth-while benefit out of the classroom, because he will never be satisfied. There is no contentment for such boys.

One cannot read such a statement without realizing Walter Camp's foresight of the true evils of professionalism. He knew what storm and strife would be aroused by his campaign against every form of it. He made the resolution strong, leaving no loopholes. He went to the convention in 1889 with the hope that the resolution would be adopted in full, and it would have been a great thing for football — and for thousands of the boys who have played it — if it could have gone through. But it was blocked by political manœuvring.

These manœuvres, which are understandable enough if you remember how bitter the competitive spirit can become, began without loss of time. Edwards of Princeton offered an amendment which would extend the ban to postgraduate students and students in all professional departments. This would have disqualified four veteran players at Harvard, at Yale, and at Pennsylvania. Leeds of Harvard countered by rising to a point of order, declaring that the call for the meeting limited the business strictly to the consideration of "certain questions of amateur standing." The chairman's ruling sustained his point. The amendment was dropped. Then Bell of Pennsylvania moved the adoption of the first part of Walter Camp's resolution, which required attendance at certain classes each week as a test of eligibility for each player. The motion was carried.

Immediately afterward, Leeds rose and with great emphasis entered a formal protest against fifteen Princeton players, on the ground that the new rule disqualified them. Princeton replied at once, filing a similar challenge against four Harvard players. The meeting abruptly adjourned at this point, to allow the challenged players to make answers.

The next session of the convention found the college representatives in something like a panic. They had canvassed the situation during the recess, and had found out what the rule would do to each squad of players. The resumption of the meeting, after Camp's earnest effort to purify the sport had been so dramatically halted by the filing of protests, was alertly watched by football enthusiasts and critics. The delegates met behind closed doors, while the hotel corridors outside were full of newspaper writers, graduates, and

self-appointed advisers who were not less zealous
because they had no official standing. This was
the first great crisis in intercollegiate football.

A motion was made to table the protest of Harvard against the fifteen Princeton players and the
retaliatory protest of Princeton against the four
Harvard men. Princeton and Pennsylvania urged
that these protests be dropped, and Harvard and
Yale resisted this solution. Wesleyan, which was
to meet Pennsylvania later in the year on the football field, hesitated for a short time, and then
aligned herself with Princeton and Pennsylvania.
The protests were therefore laid on the table.
Harvard then formally withdrew from the association, and the disintegration had begun which
was later to cause still another crisis in football
affairs.

Four years later, Walter Camp was still in tire-
less pursuit of a strict eligibility rule. He proposed, in the name of Yale, the resolution which
became known as the Undergraduate Plan.
Princeton and Wesleyan and Yale promptly accepted it, but the Pennsylvania delegates opposed
it, and when it was officially adopted the Pennsylvania membership in the football association was
withdrawn. Not long afterward Wesleyan also
withdrew, and only Yale and Princeton remained
in the association which had first sponsored intercollegiate football and had guided it through its
wonderful development. Politics had split the

association, and football was slipping down to a low place in public favor.

To cap the other difficulties, there occurred in the early 90's a series of bad accidents to players during the games. There was an outburst of public indignation. Mr. Davis has probably found the most lurid of all the comments that were made in the press. He clipped it from the *Muenchner Nachrichten,* a German newspaper which published this dispatch from the United States : —

The football tournament between the teams of Harvard and Yale, recently held in America, had terrible results. It turned into an awful butchery. Of twenty-two participants, seven were so severely injured that they had to be carried from the field in a dying condition. One player had his back broken, another lost an eye, and a third lost a leg. Both teams appeared upon the field with a crowd of ambulances, surgeons, and nurses. Many ladies fainted at the awful cries of the injured players.

This report, grotesque although its exaggerations seem, was not a bit more highly colored than were the remarks made about football by people in private life. Many a father and mother expected their son to be butchered on the football field, and the reports of injuries — magnified by their invariable appearance in newspaper headlines — only confirmed this impression. Boys were sent to school and college on condition that they would not play football. There were movements to abolish football by Act of Congress. Walter Camp met the situation sanely, by writing to all former players whose addresses he could secure, asking them to submit a list of the injuries each man had sustained. These replies, carefully tabulated, did much to calm the hysterical agitation against the game. But where there is smoke there is fire. Harvard and Princeton had already ceased meeting in football, after mutual recriminations and charges of dirty play. Yale and Harvard played a game that has been well described, in polite language, by James L. Knox of Harvard. "Yale's brilliant moments," he writes, "were when Stillman, with the game hardly two minutes old, broke through, blocked a punt, and fell on the ball for a touchdown; and again, after Thomas failed to kick a goal from the field and Harvard punted out of bounds at her own six-yard line because of Stillman's pressure on the kicker, Yale carried the ball across for another touchdown. It was not long after Yale had scored the first touchdown that Fairchild of Harvard missed a neat goal from the field, only because the ball hit the crossbar. On this same play, Waters threw Butterworth across the line for an unallowed safety. Then, in the very closing seconds of the game, Fairchild tried for another goal from the field with a perfect kick which scored nothing, because the time had elapsed just before the ball was put in play. *The outstanding feature of the struggle was the roughness of the play*, which resulted in man after man leaving the field too badly injured to return if the rules had permitted it. It did not take a great deal of foresight to realize that football between Yale and Harvard was a thing of the past, and for the somewhat distant future; and so the authorities of the two colleges ruled, with a result that all varsity sports between these two great rivals ceased after the spring of 1895. A two-year break resulted in football."

It will interest many a man who remembers this game, and remembers some of the extraordinary brutalities attributed to the men who played in it, to read Mr. Knox's restrained summary. Harvard men unquestionably believed for years, and many of them still believe, that some of the Yale men resorted to forms of mayhem that would do credit to warfare between Zulu tribes. And this feeling was reciprocated in full by Yale sympathizers who saw their players injured. Camp himself with all his conviction that Yale and Harvard undergraduates are, first of all, gentlemen, and that dirty playing defeats itself, was nevertheless impressed by the fact that, under the rules then existing, it was impossible to avoid bad blood between the players, and serious injuries. And it seemed to him, and to every other competent observer of football, a sad thing that Princeton and Harvard could not meet, and that Yale and Harvard's long friendship had turned into hate.

The old football association, in which Camp had
been the principal figure for many years, had now
melted away to a dual partnership between Yale
and Princeton. It was hard, and for the time
being it seemed impossible, for Camp to institute
the kind of reforms which he knew were necessary.
At the suggestion of the University Athletic Club
of New York, however, Yale, Princeton, Pennsylvania, and Harvard delegates met in 1894 to consider changes and improvements in the football
rules. At this conference, attention was given to
public protests against the mass and momentum
plays, which were the real source of the injuries.
Deland had contributed the fiercest principle of
momentum attack in his flying wedge, and George
Woodruff of Pennsylvania developed this principle
by working out many variations of momentum
plays. The object, of course, is to concentrate the
momentum of several interlocked players against
an oppponent, with results that are better left to
the imagination. The "flying" plays were accordingly banned. But the mass plays were left,
and they were carefully worked out by Woodruff
and other coaches. At Princeton there was the
"revolving tandem on the tackles," with which in
1896 — as Mr. Davis recalls — the team battered
out a championship. But the public does not care
about this method of battering the way to victory,
and the players themselves have a natural objection
to being battered. The game was losing its superb

kicking, its long runs, its spectacular elements of
generalship.   Camp and Deland were concerning
themselves with tandems and wedges and "funnel-
shaped alleys" through the opposing line.   They
remark somewhat bitterly in their book named
Football, which was issued at this period, that the
art of kicking had been almost lost in the preceding
years.   One description of a mass play from this
book is worth quoting, as it carries all the flavor
of football in the 90's.

Openings for mass plays [write Camp and Deland]
are not made until the push part of the play has lost its
force.   As long as the mass is moving forward, it is
utterly bad football to make any opening.   Progress
is all that is wanted, and the line men in front of the
mass should stick together, shoulder to shoulder, until
they find themselves brought almost to a standstill.
Then, with a final effort, they tear themselves apart,
carrying a break into the opposing wall through which
the runner, with the added push he is receiving from
behind and from the sides, slips, and may at times be
able to strike out for himself.

It takes no imagination to picture the great
heaving, pushing, pulsating mass of men, now
coming "almost to a standstill," now rolling and
sliding and hauling a few feet farther along, until
with its final collapse it made a huge, squirming
pile of all the twenty-two players on the field.
Such was the mass play.   It succeeded because a

team was required to gain only five yards in three
downs. These immense scrimmages were like
nothing seen on a football field before or since.

Modern eyes will find many other curious pas-
sages in this book. In those days the opposing
linemen played close together, and came to grips
like wrestlers. "If your opponent takes trifling
liberties with you, such as slapping your face,"
wrote the authors, "let all such actions merely
determine you to keep a closer watch upon the ball."
And again: "Don't fail to try to take the ball
away from an opponent whenever he is tackled.
Make a feature of this, and you will succeed oftener
than you anticipate."

But in this book, on almost every page of it,
Camp and Deland showed that they did not
blindly accept the rules as they then stood, but that
they hoped for better rules — rules that would
bring long running and kicking back into the game;
that would put emphasis on brains and not on
brawn; that would cultivate a faster, more thrilling game. "The great merit of this sport," they
wrote, "is its practically unlimited field of tactical
development. The fascinating study of new movements and combinations is never exhausted."

We may end this chapter with the obvious comment that football did not grow painlessly and
smoothly. Every new rule that helped it was
born after long and sharp argument. Every plank
and joist in the new grandstands that were being

erected — for there was no thought of building stadiums in 1896 — were paid for by men who knew that the game might be abolished utterly, at any moment. Reformers of all kinds were eager to transform football into something entirely different. There were no eligibility rules that had teeth in them. There was to come a serious dissension between the old Intercollegiate Committee and a new group of twenty-eight colleges which was to establish its own Conference Committee. The football rules prescribed — or at least, permitted — a dull and dangerous sort of game, in which injuries were far too frequent. Most of the players sincerely loathed the game, and were induced to play only by constant appeals to their college spirit. Harvard and Yale were at daggers drawn. The colleges of the Middle West were complaining that they had no place on the committee that regulated the game.

But brighter days were to come, and Walter Camp was to have an increasingly important share in bringing them about.

V

ATHLETIC TRIUMPH

In 1895 Walter Camp, on behalf of Yale, joined with Princeton in a new call for a football assembly, to which Harvard and Pennsylvania were invited. Camp and Alexander Moffatt, the great Princeton athlete who has been already mentioned as a player, were the only members remaining of the old convention. They hoped to revivify it. But it broke apart again, almost as soon as Camp and Moffatt had drawn it together. The cause of cleavage was again the mass and momentum plays. Harvard and Pennsylvania had highly developed these plays and did not wish their fairly earned advantage to be nullified. Failing to convert Camp and Moffatt to their point of view, Harvard and Pennsylvania for the second time left the council table, and Yale and Princeton were again left alone. The seceding colleges brought Cornell into their group, forming a triple league of their own. The Yale–Harvard split, however, was patched up by a special agreement between the captains of their teams.

Walter Camp had then to watch football enter a period of stress, during which it was subjected to extreme public criticism, while it lacked an authoritative directing agency. The old Football Rules

Committee had broken apart. What was left of it was regarded as unrepresentative, and as too exclusive. Some college presidents publicly challenged the committee to show by what authority it presumed to legislate upon the game. Camp and his few remaining colleagues replied that they did not seek to impose their rules upon any football teams, but were simply legislating as wisely and fairly as they could for the best interests of the game. They offered the results of their study, experience, and discussions, not as an official mandate, but as suggestions which might be accepted or rejected. This was obvious, but the criticism continued, and especially in the Middle West. The committee before long showed its appreciation of the football interest in that section by inviting A. A. Stagg, coach at the University of Chicago, to sit with the committee as delegate of that university.

The mass plays had resulted with absolute inevitability from the seemingly small change in the rules which permitted tackling as low as the knees of the man carrying the ball. Opposition to these plays continued to agitate the newspapers. They fanned the prejudices of the spectators into flame. The West Point and Annapolis teams were not allowed to play games off their respective fields. This confirmed the popular suspicion that football was a dangerous, brutal game. The West Point cadets and Annapolis midshipmen provided the most colorful of contests, and the determination of the Secretaries of War and of the Navy, backed by congressional committees, to prevent this meeting was a serious blow at football. Nevertheless, the game was being extended. More colleges and schools were playing it every year. But the game itself was dull and mechanical, with the same old piles of writhing players, the same heavy lists of casualties; and the old-time running and kicking game was superseded by short, bull-like thrusts into the middle of the line.

Characteristically enough, President Theodore Roosevelt took a hand in football in 1905. He invited Yale, Princeton, and Harvard to send representatives to confer with him at the White House about the game. This honor was not un-mixed with distressful consequences, for it aroused public interest in football, and confirmed the impression that something serious was the matter with it. Roosevelt was sincere in his statement that the game needed to be radically reformed. This stimulated all the lay critics. Walter Camp represented Yale at this White House conference, and returned from it with new respect for the President's breadth of information and sympathy with sportsmen. However, nothing of great importance came from this meeting, as a new element of discord was rapidly arising.

Chancellor Henry M. MacCracken of New York University, supported by Captain Palmer E.

Pierce, United States Army, representing West
Point, issued a call to all colleges to join in a conference regarding football. Twenty-eight colleges
responded, and from this beginning grew the
National Collegiate Athletic Association. The
first meeting was held in New York on December 24, 1905, and only Harvard among the
members of the old association sent delegates.
Captain Pierce moved the appointment by the
representatives of the twenty-eight colleges of
a new football rules committee, to be called
the Conference Committee. He suggested that
its members might sit jointly with the old
committee, if an arrangement could be reached
to make this possible. Otherwise, Captain Pierce
proposed that the new committee should legislate independently, on the authority of the new
National Collegiate Athletic Association.

An extremely delicate situation arose. Camp
knew that it would mean either a complete clipping
of his wings or else a great extension of his influence
on the game. A smaller man would have lost
the smallest remaining shred of importance. But
Camp was now to show himself the biggest man in
amateur sport. He kept cool. More than that, he
showed his honesty of purpose. He was Yale's
coach, and the greatest coach in the country, measured by results; but above and beyond that, he
was absolutely convinced that football should be
improved and continued, as a blessing for every

WALTER CAMP AT FORTY-FIVE

college which took part in it. He cordially urged the members of the old committee to join hands with the new committee. A new tribunal was formed, consisting of the members of both committees. Dennis of Cornell was elected chairman, and Reid of Harvard, secretary. Upon the resignation of Reid, two years later, E. K. Hall of Dartmouth was elected in his place. Three years later, Dennis resigned as chairman, Hall being elected to take his place. Walter Camp was then appointed secretary, and filled this position for the rest of his life. He thus emerged from the difficulty with his influence not crippled, but increased, as he was now working with a far more representative committee, and one not hampered by requiring unanimous consent to every change.

He realized, of course, that it had been his game of football which had been attacked, criticized, condemned, and denounced. Yet he was able to maintain his poise and good nature. He neither raged nor sulked when his work was attacked. Instead of resenting the intrusion of others in the effort to save the game, he welcomed their assistance. By sinking his personal feelings, he was able to accomplish what was wisest and best for the sport. From this coöperation came the compromise plan, with rules so drastically rewritten that an almost new game was played.

The forward pass was the most startling change.

Camp did not invent it. He did not approve it as an innovation. Dr. Harry Williams of Minnesota was its sponsor in the meetings, and Paul Dashiel of Annapolis supported him. But it is interesting to notice that, as soon as the pass had been made legal, Camp was the first coach who made a successful investment in it. It was like him to do that. The forward pass was lightly regarded by football tacticians, who thought of it as a last desperate resort — a sort of "shoestring" play that was more likely than not to give the ball to one's opponents. But the Yale team in the very next year, under Camp's direction, worked out a pass which was far more than a haphazard or shoestring play. Reserving it until the right moment, P. L. Veeder threw the ball to C. F. Alcott on Harvard's four-yard line, and a touchdown was the result. So Camp became the demonstrator of the scoring power of the forward pass in important games. It became in 1925, in the hands of players like Oberlander and Friedman, the most formidable of all methods of advancing the ball.

The forward pass, however, was not by any means the only output of the significant rule-making meeting in 1905. There was another provision which bears the unmistakable imprint of Walter Camp's mind. From the first appearance of mass plays, he had believed that the best way to protect the game against them was to increase the distance to be gained in order to retain possession of the ball. The close plays, the monotonous pulling and shoving and hauling, had been made possible by the absurdly short distance of five yards to be gained in three downs. Camp's plan was to increase the distance to ten yards, four downs being allowed. It was expected, quite reasonably, that long end runs must now be attempted, and that kicking would come into its own. But the forward pass nullified this hope, for the constant threat of the pass made it necessary for the halfbacks to play farther back on defense. This left the tackles and guards without quick reënforcements. The old heavy thrusts at the line were accordingly more productive of gains than before. Drives at the tackles became more profitable than ever, simply because of the adoption, in the forward pass, of a play that was designed to do away with the tackle-battering strategy.

Dr. Williams of Minnesota, who had learned football at Yale under Camp, now devised the play called the Minnesota shift. This added enormously to the pressure that could be brought to bear on any desired point in the line. Against a team not skilled in special defenses against it, the shift would develop into plays that tore through the opponent's line as if that line were wet tissue paper. And if the backfield men moved up to reënforce the line, a forward pass could easily be thrown from the shift formation. The old agitation against mass

plays was fanned again into flame. There was a
new epidemic of injuries. And in 1910 the Football Rules Committee met to purge football again,
and for the last time, of the menace of mass plays.
A radically different set of rules was adopted, so
different indeed that most spectators and old football men were unable to understand the game at
all. The officials were kept busy imposing penalties on players who were hardly better informed.
Wrote a college versifier : —

> You can talk of your backs,
> And your runners in packs,
> 　　And your quarterback speedy and tall,
> But just the same,
> In this newfangled game
> 　　It 's the referee carries the ball !

The principal changes made at this time were
the abolition of all mass plays and of interlocked
interference; the removal of linemen on offense
from positions behind the scrimmage line; the
establishment of a forward pass zone; the pro-
hibition of pulling and pushing the runner; and
various other innovations which were soon learned
by spectators and players alike.

This was a sound set of rules that was adopted
between 1905 and 1910. It has lasted, with hardly
any fundamental modification, to this day. And
there is no remaining criticism of either the brutality or the dullness of football. In every way the

game has justified the hopes that Walter Camp
had for it.   The words that he wrote in 1896 have
come true: "The great lesson of the game may be
put into a single line: *it teaches that brains will
always win over muscle.*"

After the failure of his resolution to keep graduate students off college teams in 1889, it must
have pleased Walter Camp no little to have this
matter brought up in 1905 by the faculty of the
Harvard Law School.   By this time men were
ready to go even further than he had gone.   Fresh-
men were also debarred.   The so-called "tramp
athlete" found the pickings very lean.   Yale,
Princeton, and Harvard ratified in 1906 the following agreement: —

Only such students shall be eligible for university
teams who shall have completed satisfactorily one year's
college work.

Holders of a degree advanced enough to admit at
least to the senior class of Harvard, Yale, and Princeton
respectively shall not be eligible for university teams.

No special students shall be eligible for university
teams except such as have satisfied full entrance re-
quirements, have done a full year's work, and are doing
a full year's work.

No student shall represent one or more universities
for more than three years.

The years between 1906 and 1910 were, beyond
doubt, among the happiest in Camp's life.   He
found men ready to accept the ideas for which he

had striven.   The game of football which he had
created, against many obstacles, was reformed into
the game which he had always wished to create.
And he was beginning to be known, not merely as
the most successful Yale football coach, but as the
greatest coach who has ever taught an American
team in any branch of sport.   One cannot avoid
bringing up records of games won and lost, when
appraising the value of a coach.   Figures may lie
when they are applied to only a season or two, but
they do not lie over a period of thirty years.   Read
the Yale football records, and you will find few
defeats between 1880 and 1910.   You will find
Yale winning over smaller opponents by scores
that seem grotesque if you write them down.   You
will also find Yale winning consistently over Princeton and Harvard and West Point.   This was not
mere chance, nor was it intrinsically superior
material.   It was Walter Camp.   He was not a
paid coach, nor did he even assume the title of
coach.   On the contrary, he devised the system of
giving the captain complete authority, and calling
back the captain of the previous year's team to
serve as head coach.

In the thirty years between 1880 and 1910, Yale
defeated Harvard twenty times, lost four times,
and tied three times.   There is probably no other
such record in existence of continued victory over
an opponent equal in resources.   Harvard was not
only larger than Yale, but richer.   Her men were

not, on the whole, inferior to Yale men in physique or in intelligence. Yale had to put something into the balance to secure this overwhelming preponderance. That something was Walter Camp.

From 1883 to 1910, Yale defeated Princeton twenty times, lost seven times, and tied once. It used to be said rather dismally by Princeton that each college generation saw one victory over Yale. But Princeton did not lack strong and speedy players, or good coaches. Princeton's football spirit was perhaps even better than the spirit at New Haven. Yale had something to cast into the balance and overcome all Princeton's earnestness and will to win. That something was Walter Camp.

It is pleasant to review the ways in which Camp worked as a coach — ways that seem extraordinary in the light of modern practice, but which nevertheless produced his unequaled string of victories. "I knew him," said Dean Briggs, of Harvard, "as the great master of football, whose advice — if the Yale captain would listen to it — meant inevitable defeat to the college I loved best." How this advice was often given is told by Camp himself in his own *Book of Football*. As he tells the story, he tries (with no success whatever) to disguise his own identity as "a graduate advisor." Here is the tale he tells: —

In the winter of 1899–1900, before an open fire at New Haven, with sleet and snow beating at the windows and the wind howling a gale outside, three men sat thrashing out the never-failing subject of football strategy. One was the Captain of the next year's team at Yale, the second was the field coach, and the third was a graduate advisor.

"It's the fundamentals we must work on," said the field coach. "The reason why we had such a close call last year was because we have been gradually drifting away from the good old principles of blocking your man, getting through, and tackling low. I tell you, any team that masters those fundamentals in the first month can then build up a game that will win."

"That's true," said the Captain. "We worked on other things so much that we were certainly weak in the cardinal principles."

"I agree absolutely with that," said the advisor. "But I also believe that in the general system the possibilities of offense are not half exhausted, and that a set of plays can be given a team that will simply annihilate the defense of the opponents, provided, of course, the men know straight football."

"By Jove, it would be pretty fine," said the Captain, "if we could do that."

"It can be done," said the graduate, "but it will be the hardest plan for you and the coach to carry out."

"What do you mean by that?" queried the coach.

"Because the plays will be entirely unsatisfactory to everybody while they are being put in practice. By the first of November everyone will criticize them, bemoan the time spent upon them, and predict the direst failure if they are continued."

"Do you really mean that?"

"Certainly I do, and then it will be up to you to

stand the gaff, as they say, and carry them through until they begin to have their effect. The first week they may work a little from their very novelty and because the men are interested. Then, before the individual members of the team have had sufficient practice to make them complete every movement with precision, the defense will prove the stronger. The scrub will stop the plays or tangle them all up; the team will first lose confidence, then ambition; and finally you will find even your best men, while not in rebellion, desirous of dropping the plays and going back to the simple ones upon which they have been drilled in the past."

"I can't believe that," said the Captain. "They must see that it is practice, practice that is needed."

"But that is just what they cannot believe, and even you and your coach here will be ready to abandon the plays."

"Not if you say they are good."

"Well, if my judgment of pace and the present defense is not all wrong, I am sure the plays will come out all right if you will keep at them to the end."

"We'll stick to them fast enough," jauntily returned the Captain.

"It's a bargain, then," said the graduate. "I'll lay them out and give them to you."

The winter passed, and the spring and summer. Fall practice began, and the series of plays were put into effect. They were based entirely on the theory that the opponents had been taught to play low and to charge forward immediately upon the snap of the ball. The lines of attack were so disposed as to make this very charge of each man in his line place him in such a position that, except by tremendous effort, he could not recover his balance so as to oppose effective resistance to the attack. The new plays necessitated a heavy fullback, and, no other being at hand, one of the tackles, Perry Hale, was taken from the line and made the regular fullback. Another green player was placed at tackle.

By the first of November, great was the criticism of the team. It was slow, painfully slow. A respectable end run was certainly out of the question. The back-field, to use the expression of one of the coaches, was "slower than molasses in January." Finally the Captain called up the graduate one evening and said that he thought they would have to put the fullback up at tackle again and get a faster, lighter man who could get up pace enough to keep up with the rest of the backs.

"But that means the abandonment of the plays," said the graduate.

"I know. But everyone says they never will work, and something must be done."

"Where 's McBride?" asked the graduate, naming the field coach.

"Over in his room in the hotel," said the Captain.

"I 'm going down to see him. Don't do anything till I see you later."

"All right. But things look pretty dark."

When the three men met later in the evening, it was a depressing occasion. The Captain reported that almost every man on the team had lost confidence. He had talked with them individually, and all wanted the backfield speeded up and Hale, the heavy fullback, put at his old position at tackle. The coach said that he was hearing nothing else from the coaches who had seen the game in New York against Columbia.

It was indeed a serious time, but it was finally agreed that the present positions and players should be maintained until the game with the Carlisle Indians, and if by that time and in that game they did not show their worth, the graduate was willing to see them abandoned, and Hale sent up into the line at tackle, and a faster backfield developed. Only one who has either captained or coached a football team can appreciate the feelings of these three men on the eve of the Indian game. Each knew that failure then meant too short a time to develop the team along other lines. They had virtually burned their bridges behind them, and were now to stake their season on the work of the next afternoon.

On that evening a still further chance was determined upon. The big fullback was such a factor in himself that the graduate urged an even greater hazard, but a better test of the plays. He suggested that another man, Dupee, should replace Hale for that game — a man not nearly so powerful, but one who knew the plays and would, by the experience of the game, fit himself to take the place of the fullback in the later championship games with Harvard and Princeton, should any injury incapacitate the regular man. This seemed indeed too much, but was finally accepted, and the two teams lined up.

From the very start the Yale team with its new plays marched down the field through and over the bewildered opponents, six, eight, ten, a dozen yards at a down.

The final score was 35 to 0, and the plays had made good. The Princeton game was won 29 to 5, and the Harvard game 28 to 0, and within a year half the teams in the country were playing tackle-back plays.

So Walter Camp himself raises, for a moment, the shroud of secrecy which usually hid the football councils in his day. He reveals not only the invention of these devastating plays which rolled up great scores against the most able opponents, but also shows something of the difficulty of holding, throughout a disappointing season, to a prearranged programme.

In the next year, 1902, Camp and the captain of the team, George B. Chadwick, collaborated in inventing a new twist to the tackle-back play, from which again successful scoring runs were made. Chadwick was fast and a clever dodger, able to turn instantly in his tracks and speed off in a new direction, two accomplishments of which Camp took full advantage. He designed a new play, by which all the backfield players were sent rushing off to the right, as if intent upon a "skin-tackle" thrust, with Chadwick carrying the ball and the last man to come up to the line. The interferers, in this play, were to make such a showy drive at the tackle and line, that, theoretically, the opposing defensive players would be drawn quickly over in that direction. The Yale centre and the guard were instructed to stand squarely in their places, shoulder to shoulder and immovable. Chadwick, with the ball, was to follow his interference almost to the line, then turn suddenly and drive himself against the backs of his own centre and guard. These men, holding firm, were to separate when they felt the impact of his rush, and to allow him to pass through between them with the ball.

The play, secretly developed, was held in reserve until the Princeton game was under way. Then Camp, on the side lines, heard the signal for Chadwick's surprise. He watched intently, and saw the play begin with the powerful rush at the opposite tackle. The Princeton players flung themselves out of position, toward the spot at which the Yale offensive seemed directed. Chadwick spun on his toes, plunged at the stolid centre and guard of his own line, and sprang through as they separated. A Princeton player was in the act of rushing across in front of him as Chadwick emerged with the ball in his arms. The Princeton man, seeing he had been deceived, tried to turn and threw out his arms, but he was so completely off balance that he merely succeeded in touching the flying Yale back. After that, Chadwick had only a single defensive Princeton back to elude, and he sped on for fifty-seven yards, scoring a touchdown, which overcame a five-point lead Princeton had gained through DeWitt's extraordinary fifty-yard field goal.

It is interesting here to note that George Chad-

wick performed the same feat in the second half of
that game, bursting through the Princeton line
and racing half the length of the field for his second
touchdown of that afternoon. The play on which
he scored this time seemed a repetition of the first,
and so Camp had recorded it. Remembering the
incident later, however, Chadwick said that the
second scoring play was not the same as the first,
and that he went through the Princeton line at a
spot which unexpectedly appeared. It was a for-
tuitous opportunity of which he took advantage.

Camp's ingenuity had invented this first play,
by which Chadwick was able to pass straight
through the Princeton line with only the power-
less fingers of a single Princeton player touching
him. This play defeated Princeton. Another
and a later play, in which Camp for the first time
demonstrated the effectiveness of a masked and
delayed forward pass, defeated Harvard. In the
forward-passing game, which began after the 1905
revision of the football rules, Camp and the other
coaches were faced with the problem of somehow
consuming enough time between the start of the
play and the passing of the ball by a backfield
player, to allow the eligible pass-receivers to find
their positions. Camp conceived the idea of start-
ing the play from an apparent drop-kick formation,
requiring a longer and slower pass from the player
at centre. But the time was still too short. He
elaborated the play, then, by directing the back-

field player with the ball to run backward toward his own goal before passing the ball. Again it was found that the action was too swift, and that the players who were to receive the forward pass did not have time to reach a free position. Boldly original, then, Camp suggested that the backfield player should make an apparent start at a wide, swinging end run, and halt before reaching the line in order to fling his forward pass.

The play, when first tried in secret, aroused much merriment among the Yale players. They dubbed it the "twenty-three" formation. It seemed ridiculous to them. But at the proper moment in the Yale–Harvard game, when Yale was in possession of the ball within Harvard's forty-yard line and a drop-kick seemed timely, Veeder of Yale was sent back as if to try for a goal from the field. The ball came to him on a long pass from centre, and he tucked it under his arm and started to run around the end. The Harvard team streamed over to intercept him. He ran far out toward the side of the field, so far that the Harvard defensive halfbacks were deceived into believing the play a genuine end run, and they hurried up to reënforce their linesmen. Veeder, in full flight toward the Harvard end, suddenly paused, and threw a forward pass straight into the waiting arms of Alcott, who stood alone a few yards from Harvard's goal. The entire Harvard team had been lured out of position, and Alcott found no interference as the football flew toward him. But the opportunity for a touchdown was so exciting at the moment that Alcott fumbled the ball. Later in the game, the same play was repeated and a touchdown was soon made, Alcott catching Veeder's throw on the four-yard line.

In these plays, as in many others, Camp's football genius proved itself, and his opinion of the mental process of opposing players proved correct under test. The plays, like most of those devised by Camp, were developed in hours of careful thought and in seclusion. There is no evidence that Camp, at any time, invented a football play or improvised a defense on the spur of the moment. It was his purpose to maintain himself and his team always "a jump ahead" of his opponents, and he succeeded remarkably in realizing this hope. He was not often surprised by the tactics of opponents. The appearance of the Harvard football team of 1892 in slippery leather suits, at the same time that Harvard first revealed the flying wedge devised by Deland, was probably the greatest astonishment in Camp's career as a defensive strategist. But his opinion of the leather suits, made instantly upon seeing them, was vindicated. He remarked that the suits might make it difficult to tackle the Harvard players, but that the leather would exhaust the men. This was true. The Harvard team, in the second half, had played itself out. Camp did not have an opportunity to plan a defense against the flying wedge, because one of his players, Frank Hinkey, found a way to break up the formation, by slewing its nose to one side and piling it up, before the first half was completed and therefore before Camp had a chance to speak with his men.

But his interest was far less in individual achievements, or in scores from game to game and season to season, than in the triumph of football itself. He rejoiced in Frank Hinkey, one of the most indomitable players who ever lived, too light for the game as it was played, and yet incomparable as an end. He rejoiced in all the other earnest players, from coast to coast. His voice took on a different ring when he spoke of the growth of football, of its effect on the characters of the men who played it. He quoted with pride the statement of a surgeon of Boston, who said, "Football may twist a few joints, but it is building up a new race of men." He went on to say, himself : —

"Football is essentially a game of severe moral and mental standards. No dullard can play the game successfully. Early in his career the football player will find developed in him a degree of self-reliance which probably no other sport in the world would inculcate. He acquired another and an even more valuable quality — self-control. Whatever the provocation, he must never lose his temper, never let his attention be drawn from the play. No game so tries the temper as does football. To promptness of decision and self-restraint the player must also add courage. He must have it to start with, and he will find that he has much more of it as the season advances."

He found, too, in football the great lesson of obedience : —

An army poorly officered becomes a mob; a football team without discipline would be even worse off. The player must bear the biting sarcasm of the coaches without the thought of rebellion. Every order must be unquestioningly obeyed. There are other minor advantages to the player, which must be passed over with a few words. The game requires coolness; it leads to a study of the dispositions of men, and teaches the subordination of strength to will. There is an element in human nature which finds a powerful attraction in personal contest between man and man. We cannot suppress this element, but we may wisely direct it. While in some sports it leads to cheating, it has quite an opposite effect in football. The man who loses his temper will be outplayed. The man who plays an unfair game loses more for his side than he can possibly gain.

Long after Camp wrote these words, the second most distinguished of eastern football coaches, Percy D. Haughton of Harvard, was to express the same thought in different words. Said he : —

"Sport is best carried on for sport's sake, but if you plan and aim and work to win, using everything that you have, the sport's sake will take care of itself.

Dirty playing is first of all inefficient. If you take time in a game to try some snide trick on an opponent, you are deliberately neglecting a lot of important matter that you have been told to use. To break training is the lowest form of robbing yourself and also your team of your highest performance; nothing short of your highest performance will do."

Let anyone tempted to play in a dirty way mark well these words of Camp and of Haughton. There is something higher than the mere repetition of the old proverb that "honesty is the best policy." A sportsman knows that, but he knows that honor is to be cherished for its own sake, and that defeat with honor is better than victory with any kind of trickery. Camp was the dominating character in the development of football. Some kind of football would have come into being without him, but it might have had less chivalry, less likeness to the old tournaments of knighthood, less of the color and courage and chivalry of the tourney field. All that side of football is a reflection of Camp's own character. You will find hardly another man, among all the early football players, who would have been competent to give the game the traditions it derived from him. There were other men as knightly in spirit as was Camp; but it is one thing to hold high ideals of chivalry for yourself, and another thing to teach them, as he did, with voice and pen, for forty consecutive years.

So in this chapter on the triumphs that came to Walter Camp, we must set down not merely the scores of the games which he helped to win. We must remember that he was, more than any other man, the individual who pulled the game up from the low level of sportsmanship to which it had fallen just before his time. Indeed, football had always been the black sheep of the whole athletic family. Nearly six hundred years ago, it was prohibited by King Edward III of England. In 1491, the year before Columbus sailed, King James IV of Scotland proclaimed that football must be "utterly cryed downe." Again and again, in the ages that followed, the coarse old game was banned by city ordinances. In our own colleges, before 1875, football led a precarious existence. "Unfair, brutal, drunken," were but three of the adjectives used to describe football by a college magazine in the 60's. "The game," says that report, "is won by the exercise of deliberate brutality; one may speak slightingly of bloody noses and black eyes, but we know not what is to prevent the infliction of more serious injuries."

One of the Brown College publications remarked at about the same time: "The bruised limbs, black eyes, and cracked heads are treasured as spoils of the battlefield." And the New York *Evening Post* reported that one college game of football in 1858, "were it told without one shade of exaggeration, would make the same impression on the public

mind as a bullfight.   Boys and young men knocked
each other down, tore off each other's clothing.
Eyes were bunged, faces blacked and bloody, and
shirts and coats torn to rags."

It is easy to smile at these highly colored reports,
and to take modern football for granted.   But the
man who made modern football was Walter Camp.
He rescued it from its long disrepute.   Without
him, it might still be a drunken revel, a scramble
without rules or traditions of decency.   The game
would have survived, because it is a fighting game
and man is a fighting animal.   These are the words
of Dr. Morton Prince of Boston, once a Harvard
player, and for many years one of the foremost
authorities on the human mind.

In the emergencies when modern football was
fighting for its very existence, there is no evidence
that Camp feared for it.   He foresaw what was
coming — a game purged of its old brutality, and
played under a sportsmanlike code of rules.   He
smiled when he heard that American football had
been described by an intelligent French writer as
"*cette lutte bestiale.*"   He had not played it in that
spirit, and he did not teach it in that spirit.   By
1910 he knew that the old criticisms were losing
force, and that people were accepting football just
as their grandfathers — after long anxiety and
many doubts — had accepted the railroad train.
He set himself to live and to teach in such a way
that he might be an example of what football can

do for a man. He was intellectual and not muscular; sensitive and not coarse; diplomatic and not overbearing. He was the pattern of a successful and happy man, fastidious in dress and manner, rich in friendships, and with a mind that never grew lopsided. Football held the first place in it. But he was making great headway in business, he was gaining an immense circle of friends with his pen, and he was contented in the knowledge that the football teams which he directed were far superior to their great rivals. He had known all the joys of victory. And he had consolidated all his gains; he knew more football than anyone else, and knew how to apply his knowledge.

While the games played by Yale teams were in progress, Camp sat quietly on the side lines, apparently imperturbable. He seemed ready to let the game work itself out. He could afford to be calm, for he knew everything possible in the line of preparation had been done. He had "coached the coaches." The game itself was but a demonstration of the soundness of his ideas, and of the success with which he had given them out. He had been wise, gentle, diplomatic. He had scolded and bullied no one. In all emergencies he had been like a rock upon which weaker people could lean.

He was strengthened, too, by a maxim which he had long ago borrowed from Napoleon. "In warfare the moral elements are to the physical in the ratio of three to one." Camp determined that the same thing is true in football. He said that the moral elements in football are (1) the personality of the captain or coach; (2) the ability, in Napoleon's phrase, "to seize the decisive moment"; (3) the prestige and spirit of your team; and (4) the completeness of your information about the adversary. Having made sure that these moral elements were on his side, it seemed to Camp that Harvard or Princeton would have to be three times stronger than Yale in physical resources to win, or even to tie. Such a reflection could not fail to reassure him. He said that it is only uninformed newspaper reporters and unreasoning partisans of a defeated team who raise the cry of "luck" in football. "Football games are not won or lost by luck, except in very rare instances. What appears to be luck is one of the moral qualities which, carefully nurtured by one coach and perhaps neglected by the other, proves to be the turning point in the contest." And so he went to the games with a calmness that grated upon the men around him. His poise was so perfect that it annoyed them, especially when they compared it to their own excitement. And one might conclude that he felt no emotion, and knew nothing about the usual agonies of watching a hard-fought and doubtful game. But —

George Chadwick, head coach at Yale in the season after his own graduation, went to consult

Walter Camp on the morning of the Princeton game and found him shaken and nervous. Walter Camp had outward calmness; but he had underneath, perhaps all the more poignantly because they were not expressed, the hopes and fears, the tense emotions, which other men feel and do not hide.

VI

THE DECLINE AND FALL

PRINCETON and Harvard changed their athletic coaches often, because they could not bear failure. Yale changed at last, because she could not bear prosperity.

From the standpoint of games won, no college has ever been more successful in competition with its chief rivals than was Yale between 1880 and 1910. During these years Walter Camp rose by degrees into athletic prominence at his college. As treasurer of the Yale Field Association, he became responsible for the general management and the financial side of sports at Yale. No one could wish to detract in any way from the brilliant reputations won by such other Yale athletic mentors as R. J. Cook and "Mike" Murphy. It is nevertheless true that Yale athletics, in the long period of thirty years that ended in 1910, were in the hands of Camp.

Even a glance at the record books will show what successful years they were. Yale teams were regarded as almost invincible on the football field. A victory over Yale, scored at long intervals by either Princeton or Harvard, was a cause of infinite jubilation on the part of the winners. Yale had the winning habit. Games were won, it almost seemed, before the men came out of the dressing-rooms. Many opponents went home satisfied if they had been able to hold Yale to a low score. And the example of the football teams proved infectious. At New London, for instance, Yale crews won thirteen out of fifteen races from Harvard between 1890 and 1905, and suffered but two defeats. Many of these races were hardly races at all. Yale won huge, hollow victories by such margins as seventeen lengths in 1894, and eleven lengths in 1895. It is worth observing that Harvard changed head coaches eleven times in those fifteen years, when her crews endured the long ordeal of training, only to follow hopelessly in the subsiding wash of the Yale shells. Harvard won the race in 1899, the year following Mr. Cook's retirement as coach of Yale. But to many people this victory served only to throw into relief the six consecutive Yale successes that had preceded it, and possibly to foreshadow the six consecutive Yale successes that were to follow.

Walter Camp, of course, delighted in Cook's winning record, based on thorough methods of training and teaching. Cook had made an intensive study of English rowing. His powerful crews were far more than a match for the Harvard crews. They were good enough to meet any opponents, as one of them proved by making an unexpectedly good showing at the Henley regatta in 1896. One point of likeness between Camp and Cook, differ-

ent as were their personalities and methods, may
be mentioned here. Neither of them believed in
luck. They took no stock in that modern shib-
boleth, the so-called "breaks of the game." In a
properly prepared-for game, they would have told
you, there are no breaks. Form wins. Action
equals reaction. Twice two is four.

In track athletics, Yale faced stiffer and more
intelligent opposition than in football and rowing.
But Yale won the Intercollegiate Track Championship in 1894, 1895, and 1896, and matched this
remarkable record by winning another string of
three consecutive championships in 1902, 1903, and
1904. Her teams were not only strong in reliable
first-place winners, like E. J. Clapp, '04, in the
hurdles; W. O. Hickok, '05, in the weights; and
W. R. Dray, '08, in the pole vault; but Yale was
also able to put forward men able to gain the minor
places — a sure sign of careful coaching and a large,
well-balanced squad of men. The presence of
many men who win second, third, and fourth
places does not mean that you have a poor track
team, but a good one.

Yale was never worse than fourth in an intercollegiate track meet from 1883 to 1910. Princeton finished in tenth place in 1895, behind Union
and Amherst, and has never indeed won an intercollegiate track meet since 1876, just fifty years
ago as this book goes to press. And Harvard,
despite a general impression that she always did

fairly well on the track, found six colleges ahead of her in 1907, scoring one third place and two fourth places in the meet of that year. Harvard lost the dual meets with Yale in 1901, 1903, 1904, 1906, and 1909. Only in hockey did she score with satisfactory regularity on her great rival. Baseball records are apt to be somewhat confusing; but you find Yale winning twenty-nine games from Harvard between 1880 and 1895, and losing but fifteen games — an overwhelming percentage, as such records go. Beginning in 1888, Yale won seven consecutive games from Harvard, scoring 55 runs against 18, and twice shutting out Harvard by scores of 8-o.

In any brief survey of this kind, it is hard to be either complete or fair. The reader may easily recall some great success scored by his own college team against Yale in this period before 1910. But he will surely recall that it was won against heavy odds, which made it all the sweeter. When you speak of heavy odds, you pay tribute to the skill and reputation of your foe. No college, it is certain, formed anything that approached a habit of winning over Yale. Few well-informed sportsmen, after a study of the record books, will deny that between 1885 and 1910 — the period of Camp's leadership — Yale not only had the best average football teams in the country, but also had extremely successful teams in other kinds of sport.

Sooner or later you find yourself asking the question whether victory is the chief purpose of athletics. Beyond all doubt, it *is* the purpose of intercollegiate athletics. When you play another college you play to win. Walter Camp saw to it that Yale should play to win, and Yale's record speaks for itself on the pages of the record books. Whether or not this winning habit was a blessing or a curse to Yale, is a question which this book should not try to answer. We are concerned only with its effect on Walter Camp. His final disappearance from leadership in Yale athletics was due to it. He kindled the fire, and fanned it from year to year by the success of the football teams. In the long run, he was defeated by his own success.

Some men in those winning years must have asked themselves whether Yale's reputation was to become an entirely athletic reputation. They wondered, no doubt, what these huge, thumping victories on the football field had to do with Yale's motto, *Lux et Veritas*. They may have felt that scholarship and religion must languish in an atmosphere so charged with muscular prowess and with an intense preoccupation about victory. They saw both Harvard and Princeton, to name Yale's two athletic rivals alone, growing in size and in scholastic fame, even while Yale defeated their teams on the field. Some of the truest sportsmen in America are among the professors in college faculties. These men usually feel that victory in a game is pleasant and desirable, but is not the chief purpose of the game. They may even hope that victories and defeats will balance from year to year, so that there will be more fun and uncertainty in the coming matches. But it is unusual to carry this idealistic spirit into a modern cheering section. You are thought disloyal if you do not pray and cheer for victory every time your team plays a game. Men who look philosophically at intercollegiate sports are in a slim minority. The average football spectator is carried away by emotion. He wants to win. He cannot imagine himself having a good time unless his college wins the game. It is not in ordinary human nature to sit in a stadium and smile cheerfully while the men of your own college are being beaten.

Walter Camp himself, although he was open-minded in all emergencies that affected the final good of football, was nevertheless one of the most fervent Yale partisans who have ever lived. He could not possibly be described as "a good loser," except in the superficial sense of the words. He could keep calm, of course. But his spirit hated defeat, and he planned systematically and with all his wits for victory. It is preposterous to think that he did not feel unhappy whenever a Yale team was beaten, or that he did not make up his mind that a defeat must not occur for the same reason again.

"When you lose a match against a man in your

own class," he once said, "shake hands with him; do not excuse your defeat; do not forget it, and do not let it happen again if there is any way to prepare yourself better for the next match."

You will search a long way for a better definition of the winning spirit. Camp greatly enjoyed the statement attributed to Dr. Oliver Wendell Holmes, that a gentleman in sport is a man who "plays up, pays up, and shuts up when beaten." But Camp never shut up his mind. It remained open, considering and planning football three hundred and sixty-five days a year, and never more intelligently than after one of Yale's few defeats. This is the reason that you find so few examples of an opponent scoring two consecutive victories over Yale in Camp's day.

It was a long day, but it ended in the removal of Camp. There were many reasons, but they can all be summed up into a single word — envy. If they are given here at length, it is only because they may serve to remind some other community that it is an unprofitable thing to dismiss a leader until you are sure that you have a man big enough to take his place.

Walter Camp made one mistake which helped a great deal to shorten his own career. He regarded with great satisfaction the growth of football not merely as a game, but as a spectacle. He enjoyed enormously the bustle of the crowds, the cheering, the excitement of the spectators. He was thrilled by the huge crowds he saw at games all over America, and by newspaper accounts of still larger crowds as season followed season. No wonder that he rejoiced in its success. But he forgot that these great crowds in the new stadiums that were springing up everywhere were full of people who had only the vaguest ideas of football and of sportsmanship. He thought of them as football-lovers. He thought that they understood the fine points of the game. He was eager to build an immense amphitheatre at Yale, and he expected it would be full of people who would love football in the same way that he did. He was canny enough to foresee that the money taken in from football spectators would suffice for all the other athletic expenses of the college. So his own love of football and his business judgment combined to make him overlook the fact that overwhelming popular patronage has injured every sport which it has ever touched. The crowds at the games were not the kind of crowds whom Camp had expected to welcome. It became hard for a football enthusiast to secure a seat between the thirty-yard lines. Camp spoke with pleasure of the huge crowds, and could not be persuaded for many years that it would be better for football — his kind of hard, scientific, self-sacrificing football — if the games were played on remote fields, with no grandstands, and with only a few hundred spectators, limited to men who had played the game themselves.

Football crowds, as the game leaped into public favor, turned out to be the same kind of crowds who must have filled the Coliseum at Rome — sensation-lovers who wanted a great spectacle, and loved the throngs and the music and the colored flags and balloons; raging partisans, who had betted on their team without real knowledge of its ability; girls who took it for granted that their escorts would get them seats for The Game — a vast, motley, cheering crowd, reeking with perfume and alcohol, and full of an intense lust for victory.

Here and there in such crowds are plenty of men, and not a few women, who really love football. Too often, in the present demand for tickets, you find them seated behind the goal posts, or unable to get inside the gates at all. The great mass of a football crowd includes people who have never played the game, never read the rules, and who are chiefly attracted by a warped sense of college loyalty, or by a desire to see some famous player in action.

Such a crowd is a very interesting thing, but it can also be a very dangerous thing. It gives the players a false sense of their own importance. It is blindly eager for victory. It has no mercy on a beaten eleven, or on a man who makes some mistake that loses a game. It has no pity on a coach whose team loses a championship. It has called into being, indeed, a race of coaches who are migratory and who flit from one college to another.

There is no other occupation in which one failure can wreck a career more thoroughly. But the real wrecker is the big, unthinking crowd which cares much less for football than for football victories.

As Walter Camp grew older, it was natural enough for younger men to feel that his ideas were obsolete. These younger men overlooked the fact that Camp himself had been the chief developer of "modern" football. They knew that, as a player, he had never been allowed to use the forward pass. It seemed incongruous that he should now be able to teach it, or to devise plays built around it. There is always the hope, on the part of a crowd of people who do not know football, that some trick play or series of trick plays, can defeat an opposing team. Walter Camp came to be regarded, unfairly, as an old fogey; a man who resisted progress, whose football was of an antiquated kind. The mere fact that he sometimes, between 1900 and 1910, came down to the field during practice, and took off his coat, and plunged into something that closely approached real play, was so remarkable on the part of a middle-aged man that it lent emphasis to the remarks of those who said he was growing old.

His own system of coaching, in which last year's captain returned as field coach and directed the season's play along with the new captain, was an ideal one until the new complexities of the game demanded a permanent (or apparently permanent) head coach. This old Yale system, with Camp himself to back it up as advisor, won for Yale a steady succession of victories from 1902 to 1908. A defeat came seldom in those years. And every year there graduated from Yale many men well trained in football — men who proved themselves highly successful as coaches at other colleges, and who naturally regarded themselves as competent to coach at Yale.

If Camp made a preventable mistake in allowing football to be overemphasized on the part of the general public, he made at about this time another mistake which he could not prevent. He allowed himself to be thought of as cold. He was no more capable of false joviality than George Washington himself was capable of it. Like James J. Storrow, "he shook many hands, but he never shook one for the sake of a vote or a favor." As an undergraduate, he had always been ready for any wholesome fun. He had tolerated all kinds of men who were his inferiors, playing games with them despite his own great superiority, associating with them frankly and freely for the sake of human companionship. But there is no doubt that he stiffened as he grew older. He made new friends slowly. He reserved his good fellowship, his quick sympathy, and his sunny good humor for those old friends who had proved themselves worthy. He was not a hero worshiper. Some of the younger football heroes, in his later years, may have thought him intentionally cold to them. His interest was always in the team, not the man. He believed with Kipling that : —

> The game is more than the player of the game,
> And the ship is more than the crew.

Camp played no favorites. It was thought by a few that he was taking credit for plays invented by other men. As a matter of fact, he was taking deserved credit for victory, not for its details. He was running, very gently and in an inconspicuous way, a school of football which constantly created new ideas. He prepared the soil from which heroes sprang. It could not be expected that they would give him full credit for their education. To young men who came and asked his advice, he was uniformly patient and helpful. One of them was S. H. Philbin, for three years a halfback until his graduation in 1910. Philbin haunted Camp's house, interfering with bridge games and with Camp's other hours of leisure. It was in this way that he learned to play football well, and Camp acquired a lasting respect for him. But not all the young men were so ambitious or so teachable. Many of them failed to understand that Camp was either teaching them or managing the system that enabled other men to teach them.

As time went on, and they won games with regularity, they began to give themselves most of the credit. Football makes heroes — young, unthink-

ing, immature and unbalanced heroes. Like every
other winning team, each Yale team contained at
least one young man whose self-importance was
titillated by the applause of the crowds, and the
hero-worship of the campus, and the presentation
of his name in newspaper headlines. This kind of
thing goes to the twenty-year-old head. It would
go to the forty-year-old head just as quickly, perhaps. It takes a level-headed football hero to
walk modestly. There have been such men —
Gordon Brown, for example, or Marshall Newell —
but there have not been very many of them. It
is easy to make a run through a hole in the line and
afterward to forget all about the hole. It is not
customary in football reporting to say: "Smith
and Robinson made a large hole and a touchdown
was scored." The report usually reads: "Green
plunged over the line for a touchdown, winning
the game."

Green and his friends are pretty sure to be
affected by this kind of report, if it is often repeated. A boy remembers his fifty-yard run, and
forgets the interference that made it possible. He
remembers giving a signal for a play that scored a
touchdown, but he may forget who invented that
play and told him at what moment to use it.

Walter Camp never thought it wise to give excessive credit to individual players. In fact, he
was extremely reticent of personal praise, except
after the close of each season, when he chose his

All-America Team. Even then his interest was more in the team than in the individuals. It is fair to say that he often disappointed young players who would have greatly appreciated receiving his praise. It must not be thought that he could have staved off his dismissal, and courted false popularity, by being hypocritical. It was not in him. He could not have assumed any geniality which he did not feel. His honesty was transparent. It was no part of his business to flatter young men. He could and did seem to them, on occasions, very stern and unsympathetic. And there were many times when he disagreed sharply with younger men, and did not pay them the compliment of explaining his reasons. He hated soapbox oratory, which is so often called freedom of speech. The loose-mouthed sort of man found him a poor listener.

He carried a heavy responsibility as dictator of Yale athletics, and he showed that he knew it. The peculiar Yale football coaching system was only practical when the captain — to whom such complete authority was delegated — was cool and mature enough to know that he was no autocrat at all. He derived all his authority from Camp. If serious disagreement arose, either he or Camp would have to go. Systems last only as long as men agree to make them last. It may have seemed to Yale men that the football system was a perfect and durable thing, which would last as long as the college itself. Actually, as Camp well knew, the system would vanish as soon as one captain proved himself a mutineer.

Many men wanted Camp's scalp. Had they stopped to reflect, they would have known that the mere threat of Camp's presence somewhere behind the Yale team was worth, let us say, one touchdown a game. "Exchange kings," said the Irish, after the Battle of the Boyne, "and we will fight you again and beat you." The mere threat of Napoleon's presence on a battlefield was said to be worth fifty thousand men in its moral effect on an enemy. Yale's opponents had similar ideas about Camp. They regarded him as the man who invented Yale's successful methods. Even if this impression had been wrong, it nevertheless was present. But many Yale men were too confident and too careless to verify it. The most superficial investigation at Princeton and at Cambridge would have taught them that the one great gleam of hope which football men in those institutions could pray for would be the removal of Walter Camp. But no! Such an event was not even dreamed of. Harvard and Princeton had no knowledge of the great stroke of good fortune that was coming to them.

And the Yale men who sought Walter Camp's dismissal were not disloyal to Yale. They really believed that they knew more football than he did. The memory of the games in which he had been a

player was growing dim.   But the younger men recalled their own games, and forgot that in preparation for them they had learned — under Camp —
more football than most players will ever know.
A player on one of these winning Yale teams was
sure of a coaching job at another college if he cared
to accept it.   Again the question arose: Why
could he not have the honor and glory of being
head coach at Yale?

We may be sure that if any one of these detrac-
tors of Camp had known that the football systems
at both Princeton and Harvard were going to be
greatly improved, his loyalty to Yale would have
kept him from attacking Camp.   A few years
later, when Yale's teams were demoralized and
Yale was passing through the most harrowing
seasons of defeat that ever came to a first-rate
college, it was easy to see the havoc brought about
by the departure of Camp.   But the young men
were not able to read the future.   They were sure
that Yale would prosper even more in athletics
without Camp's services than with them.

By 1907 and 1908 the stage was set for a
revolution.   The hot water was coming to a boil.
Yale had twenty or more famous players, many of
whom were eager to take the coaching reins.   It
seemed needless to submit any longer to the old-
fashioned ideas of the aging prophet in the clock
company — a prophet without honor in his own
country!

And then a very disturbing thing happened. The Yale team in 1908 was hardly one of Yale's best elevens. There were considerable cavities in the positions where such men as J. J. Hogan and E. T. Glass and R. C. Tripp had played. There were two stars in the backfield, but two men do not make a modern football team. After a not too promising early season, this team met Princeton and was badly beaten in the first half. Largely by the efforts of Coy and Philbin, the team rallied in the second half and managed to win.

But sharp eyes had probed its early-season weaknesses, and a new coach at Harvard was preparing to take advantage of them. He was an untried man, Percy D. Haughton, who had spent one autumn coaching at Cornell, and had served in a minor capacity on previous Harvard coaching staffs. He was no match for Camp in experience, but he came very near to being a match for him as a student of the game. His innovations at Soldier's Field were all practical. For instance, there had been only one tackling dummy for the squad, so that hours were wasted while each man waited for his chance to use it. Haughton installed six dummies. He remarked grimly to his men that a football season is a matter of hours, and not of months, and that he proposed to use each minute to the full. Haughton's victories were all due to this insistence on hard facts. It is not believable that he expected to beat Yale in that first year of his coaching. But he did.

He faced Yale at New Haven with a Harvard team which had tied Annapolis, and had succeeded in reversing bad defeats inflicted during the year before by Carlisle and by Dartmouth. The Harvard line was not the sluggish line it had been in former seasons. Coached by Graves of West Point, the men played with a certain "frightfulness" which was allowable under the existing rules. The backfield men were well drilled in simple plays; and there was an end, G. G. Browne, who could be depended on to catch punts and not fumble them, thus removing one of the possible breaks of the game. But Harvard suffered a serious loss on the eve of the game, due to injuries which kept its best player and captain, F. H. Burr, out of action.

Despite Haughton's sensible preparations, the Yale team would have won by a moderate score had not Harvard's quarterback, Cutler, been able to exploit the temporary weakness at one end of the Yale line. This weakness lasted just long enough for Harvard to carry the ball forward into a position from which V. P. Kennard, a substitute, scored a field goal. For the rest of the game Harvard was called on to resist the same kind of attack which had overcome Princeton a week earlier. At one time, another good kick — this time a punt, by H. B. Sprague — took Harvard out of a perilous situation on her own goal line. But Yale's great chance came when her quarterback, J. F. Johnson, ordered a surprise forward pass from a position twenty yards in front of the Harvard goal. To Walter Camp, listening for the signals on the side lines, this seemed the most critical moment in the game. A touchdown would wipe out Harvard's lead, and would restore Yale's spirit.

On receiving the ball, Johnson ran backward and to one side. Turning, he sent the ball spinning over the scrimmage line.

William S. Langford, veteran official, watched the play and knew that it was the turning point in the game. The rules required the ball to pass over the scrimmage line at least five yards on one side or the other of the point at which the play began. As the Yale quarterback let the ball fly from his hand, Langford marked its flight and ran forward, blowing his whistle. The ball had passed through the prohibited zone. A Yale man caught it, and fought his way to Harvard's five-yard line before he was downed. Had the pass been allowed, it would have placed the Yale team in a perfect position from which to score. But the pass went for nothing, and the game ended with Harvard leading, 4–0.

Walking off the field, Langford met Camp in the dark tunnel which led under the old grandstand on Yale Field.

"What was the matter with that forward pass?" demanded Camp.

Langford briefly explained why he had recalled the ball. On the Monday morning after the game, he found on his desk the letter that follows: —

NEW HAVEN, *Nov.* 24, 1908

Dear Mr. Langford:

I just drop you this line in case you have not seen the statements in the newspapers made immediately after the game.

I took pleasure in writing in my article that night for the newspapers, and Coach Biglow also said, as did I believe also one or two others, that there could be no question whatsoever about the accuracy of your decision on the forward pass and that you were in a position to see and that you caught it previous to its being caught by Brides.

I wish to thank you for your work in the game, which was first class. With best wishes, believe me, very truly yours,

WALTER CAMP

This letter is in attractive harmony with Camp's ideal of sportsmanship. He had feared that his abrupt question, in the gloomy tunnel leading under the field, might have caused Langford to think he was complaining. Complaint against a decision, no matter how close or how important, was abhorrent to Camp. Therefore he took care to inform the referee that he considered the decision right and fair. Not many men would have done so. Yet that decision contributed indirectly to the end of Camp's career as graduate advisor of football teams at Yale.

Every lover of football must regret that Haughton and Camp were pitted against each other only twice. Harvard won the first of those two games and Yale the second. Haughton was obliged to do quickly what had taken Camp a lifetime — that is, to develop a sound and enduring football system. Nobody can tell what might have happened if Haughton's great elevens of 1914 and 1915 had met teams coached by Camp. It is sufficient to say that these men had great respect for one another, and that the games which were played in those years suffered, from a Yale standpoint, by the absence of Yale's great strategist.

However, it is not necessary to tell here about the gloom that fell upon Yale football after Camp retired, nor should the details of his withdrawal be given. His work was done. And it was not only in preparing football teams, and in sowing the seeds of victory in other sports, that this work was effective. As treasurer of the Yale Field Association, he had saved its funds religiously from year to year; it is an extraordinary tribute to the Yale spirit of mutual confidence that no accounting was demanded. When Walter Camp came forward at last with a fund of $135,000, there were indeed a few men who thought he was laying too much stress on the commercial side of athletics. But these objections disappeared when he explained

that this fund might not only help to build a worthy
and safe arena for football games, but would help
such sports as rowing, from which no revenue can
be derived, and also the freshman sports, and so-
called minor sports, that are so beneficial to the
players, but which cannot earn their own way.
Such sports had previously been supported by a
burdensome system of taxes (miscalled subscrip-
tions) levied upon the undergraduates. Now
Walter Camp pointed out that this levy could be
abolished. He had a very clear vision of the great
modern football arenas that will seat more than
fifty thousand spectators and will provide almost
unlimited revenue for all worthy athletic purposes.

Camp's resignation from all official connection
with Yale athletics came in 1910. He retired after
long and anxious thought, with the conviction that
this action would be best for Yale. In this conclusion, as many Yale men tried to persuade him
during the remaining years of his life, he was seriously mistaken. He consented, after much pressure, to come down to the practice field occasionally, and to advise the coaches and captain. But
the old system disappeared with him, and the
amazing series of Yale victories disappeared too.
It was the end of a régime and a dynasty — the
beginning of anarchy and defeat. Never again
was Walter Camp to serve upon any Yale committee for the teaching or the administration of
sports.

VII

THE LAST TOURNAMENT

THE decay in Yale athletics, which set in after Walter Camp's retirement as chief advisor to the football teams, came so rapidly that it can be summarized by the scores of the games. In 1911, a scoreless tie was played with Harvard. In 1912, Harvard won by 20–0, in 1913 by 15–5, in 1914 by 36–0, and in 1915 by 41–0. Such victories tell their own story of an increasing confidence on the part of Harvard, and of growing demoralization at Yale. There were seasons after, not only Princeton and Harvard but many other colleges discovered that Yale had softened and was ripe for defeat, when many Yale men were almost unwilling to pick up their newspapers and read the score of the game on the day before. Instead of giving these scores at more length, it may be permissible to quote some lines in which the Harvard *Lampoon* showed that it was well known in Cambridge why Yale, minus Walter Camp, was traveling so rapidly to defeat. The lines are addressed to Dean Briggs. They begin with the statement that Yale's athletic supremacy is dead and buried. From this point they continue : —

Gabriel's Trump could not awake her, she will never reappear
Undefeated, as we knew her, when she held her title clear

To the great blue-bosomed triumph stretching on from year
   to year

In those years of Yale's abundance ere she loosed her iron
   clamp
Who prepared her gaudy conquests, who around the evening
   lamp
Coached the coaches at New Haven?   We remember Walter
   Camp —

Cool, resourceful, cunning, patient.   Dimly might we then
   discern
Any hope to break the shackles; still you bade us live and
   learn,
Never doubting right would triumph, or the longest worm
   would turn.

After thirty years of glory, full of honor and renown,
Camp went back to making clockworks and the star of Yale
   went down!
Princeton beat her soft elevens, so did Colgate, so did Brown.

Wash. & Jeff. harpooned her freely; Boston knocked her
   for a goal;
Harvard's annual performance must have warmed your iron
   soul
When the frog-like chorus faltered in their horror-haunted
   Bowl.

Amid the clamor of such balladry, and the con-
sternation of sports writers who had been taught
by long experience to regard Yale teams as almost
invincible, it was known to most people that
Camp's hand was no longer on the wheel, and that
Yale had dropped the pilot.

In point of fact, Camp came occasionally to Yale Field after his retirement, but he came without his old authority. He was like a retired general who may be allowed to visit headquarters but who is not entrusted with even a shred of command. A force had departed.

George Chadwick tells in a letter how most Yale men regarded Walter Camp during the thirty seasons when he was the great intelligence behind Yale's teams : —

Whatever may have been my personal ideas about college football, and the lack of balance in the prominence given it [writes Mr. Chadwick], I nevertheless had a job to do at New Haven when I was captain, and I thought seriously enough about it. Walter Camp had at that time no official position in connection with Yale football. In those days the captain was boss. But he was there to use, if one wanted him, and I sought him out deliberately as the greatest aid a Yale captain could have. I have been trying to recall colorful incidents about Camp, and I can't, except for the one I have already related to you — my call at his office on the morning of the Princeton game the year I was coach, the extreme nervousness he showed, and my surprise and pleasure in it; for I had never seen him nervous before and I was delighted to find that he was human after all.

What does stand out in my mind is a sort of hovering force, that wisely and unobtrusively guided me in my thoughts and actions: a force that held an amazing amount of football knowledge, and the benefit of the

whole Yale football tradition — a tradition in those
days certainly of football success.   If one may call a
man a force, I should like to pay tribute to Walter
Camp as that force.

I am not thinking of eulogizing him.   I don't like
biographies that merely eulogize, and I hope your
biography of Camp will not be that kind.   The more
clearly and honestly a biographer puts before you both
the faults and virtues of a man who has accomplished
things, the better the man emerges in his true power.
But I have searched my memory, and I can find nothing in my contact with Camp that in any way shat-
tered the high ideals of youth, or that emphasized
wrong ideals or impractical ideals.   The college boy is
an idealist, full of unselfish devotion.   It is my remem-
brance that Walter Camp sanely fostered this idealism
in his contact with young men.   He was out to win —
which is a good thing to foster, too.   But he was never
out to win, so far as I can recall, by any evasion of the
rules or of the spirit of fair play.   He often said to me:
"We must always be just a little ahead of the other
fellow," and he continually brought up many minute
details of play, any one of which might mean the difference between victory and defeat.   Football was, I
believe, the background of Camp's whole life.   And
yet, what he expressed through his football interest
was a much bigger thing than a mere constructive
interest in a game.   If one impresses himself as Camp
did, the medium matters little.

I have been reading further in *Lord Jim* and have
come to the elderly French lieutenant.   Conrad's
description of him makes me think of Camp.   It reads:

"His imperturbable and mature calmness was that of
an expert in possession of the facts, and to whom one's
perplexities are mere child's play." When I knew
Camp he had reached a wise maturity, but he did n't
give you the feeling that your perplexities were child's
play but were of importance — which is better.

In that period of my life Walter Camp was a real
and good influence. So must he have been to many
other Yale men, similarly placed. And the fact that I
rarely think about football nowadays does n't make his
influence of less present value. What is genuine and
true lasts most surely.

The removal of the force that was Walter Camp
from Yale's football coaching had an effect not
only on the football teams, but on the other teams.
Victory is infectious, and defeat is more so. Harvard won the baseball series from Yale in 1911,
1913, 1915, and 1916; still more surprisingly, on
account of past records, Harvard won the race at
New London for six consecutive years, beginning
in 1908. Yale won no intercollegiate track meet
between 1908 and 1916, during which period the
championships were monopolized by Cornell and
Pennsylvania, with a single victory for Harvard.
Yale did win five dual track meets from Harvard,
between 1909 and 1916, and lost only three; this
was practically Yale's only success in major sports
between Camp's retirement and the World War.
Yale won the hockey game from Harvard in 1908,
only to lose thirteen out of the next fifteen games.

The suggestion has been made that Camp found a certain grim satisfaction in Yale's defeats during this period. This is a lie. He suffered as much in spirit as any other loyal Yale man. It was said that Yale had ceased to be a virile, athletic college, and was becoming addicted to literary æsthetics. And this too was false. Yale had never been primarily an athletic college, and her sudden interest in literary things would have come about whether her athletic teams were winning or not. But these teams had won constant successes while Camp was at the helm, and the slump began as soon as he withdrew. He viewed it with genuine sorrow. Certain Job's comforters tried to suggest to him that victory and defeat come in cycles. He could not agree, believing that victory comes because you prepare for it, and so does defeat. Camp had shown that, under intelligent leadership, it is possible to win games continually for a period of thirty years. If that is a mere swing of the pendulum, it is a long swing. He knew that nothing succeeds like success, or fails like failure. The "cyclic" theory of competitive athletics is a delusion.

It was never necessary for Walter Camp to prove his intense loyalty to Yale; but in the years of athletic famine through which Yale was now passing he had abundant opportunity to prove his sportsmanship. Each year he reviewed the season for the *Official Football Guide*. He made no reference to the obvious fact that Yale teams were

poorly coached. On the contrary, he paid tribute to the improved coaching at Harvard, under
Percy D. Haughton, and he rejoiced in the order
which W. W. Roper brought into Princeton's
affairs after the war. And whenever a first-rate
Yale player appeared on Yale's ill-prepared and
ill-fated teams, Camp paid him generous homage.
For instance, he selected for his All-America Team
such great players as J. R. Kilpatrick, D. M.
Bomeisler, H. H. Ketcham, and N. S. Talbott.
These men struggled valiantly in the face of defeats
of a kind that had never come before to Yale.
Camp recognized their quality and published
it. A great player is often made doubly great
by the presence of a good team all around him.
These men, notably Ketcham and Talbott, were
obliged to play under great handicaps, and without the satisfaction of victory. But Walter Camp
recognized their ability, and gave them the greatest distinction which remained in his hands to
bestow.

A man of the petty type would have grasped
the opportunity that Camp had at this time. He
could have readily attributed Yale's failures to
his own absence from headquarters. But he kept
himself free from meanness. He was called a
"has been." He might have retorted that it was
better to be that than a "never was." But he
did not make such retorts. It is significant that
he came through the period in which he lost his

athletic prominence at Yale without losing the respect of his associates.

He served as usefully as ever on the Football Rules Committee after 1910, although the sweeping reforms which had been made in that year and in the preceding years had removed the old public hatred of the game and the need of sweeping reforms. Every year he improved the new game which his unthinking critics believed he did not understand. He went to as many games as ever, traveling widely to do so, and collecting each year an increasing amount of data for use in football legislation, and for guidance in selecting his All-America Team. Once it had been merely necessary to watch the old "Big Four," together with Chicago, Michigan, Cornell, Illinois, and a few others. But now Camp found it necessary to have eyes in California and in the South. Nothing in his career was more mysterious to the public at large than the All-America Team. It appeared originally as a journalistic feature in *Collier's Weekly*. The first team, in 1889, included (as you will find in Appendix A) five Princeton men, and three each from Yale and Harvard. But it was not for long that these teams were to monopolize either Camp's attention or the best football players in the country. Pennsylvania, Cornell, Carlisle, Chicago, West Point, Columbia, Dartmouth, and Michigan soon contributed men to the teams. A little later you find Pennsylvania State College,

Nebraska, Indiana, Wisconsin, Lafayette, and Minnesota players on the three teams which Camp picked. Holy Cross and Notre Dame soon followed, and presently there were men from Vanderbilt, Alabama, Oregon, California, and others.

The All-America Team proved extremely popular. It was regularly copied on the sports page of practically every newspaper that had a sports page. The name became a household word. It was not by any means the first household word that Camp coined nor was it to be the last. Remember "quarterback" and "Daily Dozen." But there were countless imitations: All-Eastern Teams, All-Western Teams, All-Scholastic Teams, and many more. The Walter Camp All-America Football Teams, indeed, gave great impetus to the modern mania for picking the twelve immortals in literature, the fifty best books in the world, the six greatest men who have ever lived, and the other lists of this kind which are now so common. (The purist may notice that the word is "All-America." It is usually misspelled, "All-American.")

Any list which wins popularity also courts criticism, and the critics of the All-America Teams from year to year finally reached the conclusion that it was impossible for Camp to see all the different teams play (which was true), and that he could not accordingly pick the best men (which was false). For he quietly organized a remarkable system of reporting. His correspondents saw all the players, and reported to him systematically throughout the season. These assistants included many coaches who had played with Camp, or been taught by him. There were also many former players who kept up their interest in the game, and not a few newspaper men who really knew football. They took their duties very seriously. "In twenty-four years of football at Michigan," said Fielding H. Yost, "I recommended only eleven Michigan players. I recommended only men of the type of Heston, Schulz, Benbrook, Craig, and others who were outstanding stars, men of unusual ability and character."

From the enormous mass of notes that came to Camp, he selected at the beginning of each season a squad of perhaps one hundred men. Then, from week to week, on the ground of supplementary recommendations and from his own observation of the players whom he watched in practice, and in the most important games of the season, Camp cut this squad down on paper, just as he would have cut it down on the field. He thought nothing of traveling hundreds of miles to see a single player. At the end of the season, he had his first, second, and third teams. He always thought of the All-America as a team, and not merely as eleven star players. For instance, in 1899 he wrote: —

"If it be luck that has enabled this young man (Poe of Princeton) to win two games from Yale,

The Yale Graduates' Team which played an exhibition game at the Yale Bicentennial in 1901. Top row, left to right: J. Hall, W. Wright, R. Townsend, S. L. Coy, P. T. Stillman, R. Hickok, B. C. Chamberlin, F. Murphy, J. C. Greenway, H. Cross, P. K. W. Hale, W. H. Corbin, W. W. Heffelfinger, A. H. Sharpe. Middle row: Gordon Brown, G. B. Cutten, R. Armstrong, G. Hutchinson, F. S. Butterworth, S. B. Thorne, Walter Camp, *Captain*, O. D. Thompson, M. Ely, C. Chadwick. Front row: Lee McClung, Vance McCormick.

then his luck is worth adding to the national team, if only for superstition's sake. Besides, we may want a man who can kick a goal under extreme pressure."

He writes "we may want," which shows as clearly as anything can that be regarded the All-America as a team preparing to play a game. It may console many men who did not find their names upon it to know that Camp never said that it contained the eleven best players in America. There was never room for two centres, or three guards or tackles. In very rare cases, room was found for a peculiarly versatile player by putting him in a position not regularly his own. In 1904, for example, he chose eleven men for the team, with Stevenson of Pennsylvania as quarterback. But there was at Chicago a brilliant star, whom Camp regarded as only slightly inferior in that year to Stevenson. "Regarding Eckersall," he wrote, "I have placed him at end, only after choosing all the rest of my team, and endeavoring to put myself into the position I should assume as coach and were I faced with the responsibility of selecting from the array of material a man who would serve me best on the team as it went into actual play. Weede of Pennsylvania, Gillespie of West Point, and Glaze of Dartmouth all would suit me well for a mate to Shevlin at end. But I believe that these men (and I know something of their unselfishness on teams) would, if threatened with the actual situation, agree with me in preserving my back-field intact, and securing a kicker by placing the marvelous kicker, and brilliant tackler and runner, Eckersall, on the other end next to Hogan."

Camp had chosen a backfield quartet brilliant in everything except kicking. Rather than disrupt it, he went past three regular ends whose perform-ances had certainly entitled them to a position, and elected as his second end a backfield player whose kicking ability would help the team. And Camp appealed on the ground of loyalty and sportsmanship to three great players he had dis-appointed, knowing that they were big enough to understand his reason. Weede and Gillespie and Glaze were All-America men in 1904. Their names are not on the team, but Camp saw to it that their unselfishness would not pass without notice. In the following year one finds Eckersall at his regular position of quarterback, while Glaze has been placed at end.

Comparatively few men ever "made" Walter Camp's All-America Team for two years or more. Among them are such football immortals as Frank Hinkey (4 years), W. W. Heffelfinger (3 years), Truxton Hare (4 years), W. Heston (2 years), John De Witt (2 years), T. L. Shevlin (3 years), and E. W. Mahan (3 years). Walter Camp chose no man on account of past reputation, but only on the basis of each season's play. He agreed with

Grantland Rice that "it is n't what you used to be, it 's what you are to-day."

The writer of this book sat with Walter Camp twice while the final selections were made, on the evenings after the West Point–Annapolis games. It was evident that Camp had no prejudice in favor of either Western or Eastern teams. He went entirely by the records of the players. He had a battery of small, technical, telling facts about each man, the little details of technique that only a trained observer can see. He made no effort to flatter eleven colleges by choosing a man from each one. In fact, he seemed to have forgotten all about the colleges, as he concentrated on the players. From his huge bundle of neatly classified and annotated notes, he picked a quarterback who he thought would be best fitted to direct the play of the team, and three other backs who would fit best with that quarterback and with one another. He made sure that he had not only a good kicker, but also a reserve kicker who could do well enough in an emergency. He was proceeding by the same careful methods through which, in the old days, he welded the Yale team together. He had no time for any other considerations. He was not thinking about different colleges, or about different sections of the country. For instance, if the Vanderbilt or the Dartmouth team had included the best man for every position, he would not have hesitated to name the whole eleven.

It was this scrupulous judgment, which spoke for itself when the team came to be published, promptly at the close of each season, that made its success. He published it in *Collier's Weekly* each autumn, out of a fine sense of loyalty to that periodical, although he could for a long time have sold it for more money to a newspaper syndicate. As a feature which every newspaper liked to print, it had a very high market value. Once, indeed, a thievish visitor to the shop in which it was printed actually stole the list, and tried to sell it in advance of its regular date of publication. To prevent this, the list was split up into three short "takes," which were assembled just before the weekly magazine went to press. This was an extraordinary precaution, but it was justified by the widespread interest in the team.

Walter Camp took a great deal of pride in his All-America Teams, and in the fact that no rival selections were successful in his lifetime. A magazine once hit upon a plan that seemed workable. Its editors sent letters to leading sports writers all over America and invited them to pick the best possible teams from their own observation and knowledge. Then a composite team was chosen, by listing the votes given to each player. Walter Camp looked at this team with interest.

"Those are eleven good men," he said, "but the captain will be sorry to find out, in the game, that he has nobody who can kick the ball."

None of Walter Camp's All-America Teams has a deficiency of this kind. Each is fitted to play the best kind of winning football that was known in its year. The men who were chosen are rightfully proud of the distinction. One autumn, a great player was taken ill soon after the close of the season; in fact, it was thought that by too strong loyalty to his team mates he had insisted on concealing his true condition, and had played after becoming conscious of the symptoms of serious illness. A man who greatly admired this player wrote and asked if his name were included on the All-America Team. Receiving an answer, he took the trouble to make a long journey to his bedside and to give him the news. Even at that moment, it brought joy to the dying man.

For a great many years Camp picked the All-America Team with increasing satisfaction and pleasure. He did not stop to calculate its cost to him, or he would have found that it was costing him much more than he was receiving for it. The All-America helped to make everyone realize his position at the head of football in this country, and it allowed him to play football games mentally. The strain of "coaching the coaches" ended in 1910, but for fourteen years more he had the pleasure of sifting a large squad of the best players and of outlining in his mind the games they would play against their opponents. He was a man of uncanny judgment in picking winners, not in football alone, but in all the other games he watched.

For instance, after many years of almost undisputed supremacy in court tennis, Jay Gould took up squash tennis and met the champion in that game, Fillmore Hyde, in a match for the title. For some time, Gould played Hyde off his feet. His great experience in court tennis, the force of his competitive personality, and the great brilliancy of his shots all made the spectators feel that he would win. But before the match was five minutes old, Camp whispered to his neighbor that Hyde was safe. Asked for his reason, he said that Hyde had a way of pivoting easily on his hips and could therefore put great force into what seemed an easy stroke; while Gould, less accustomed to the angles in the small court, was hitting largely with his arm muscles, and would surely feel the strain toward the end of the match. The result more than justified Camp's comment.

At about the same time, Camp attended a national golf tournament, played in Pennsylvania. He walked over the course one afternoon, noticing the depth and construction of the hazards. "I am looking for a big, well-muscled man, with large and strong forearms," he wrote on a postal card that evening to a friend. "Nobody else can stay this course in this heat." The general opinion was that Evans or Jones would win. A day or two later, however, Camp wrote the name "Herron"

on another postal.   Evans and Jones did not meet
his physical specifications, but Herron did.   He
was the darkest kind of a dark horse; but on that
course, and in that weather, he defeated Jones and
won the championship.

The classic story, however, of Camp's ability to
observe small details and to make accurate deduc-
tions is one often told by Lorin F. Deland.   In
1896, Yale and Harvard did not meet in football,
and Princeton met Harvard at Cambridge.   Camp
and Deland had been working together on their
textbook, *Football*, and they naturally took side-
line seats together at the game.   Harvard was
out for revenge against Princeton, which had won
the year before by virtue of a tremendous run of
one hundred yards by H. M. Suter — one of the
longest ever seen on a football field.   After ten
minutes of play, Camp made the flat statement to
Deland that Princeton would win again, basing
this statement upon his observation that Princeton
was trying to score, while Harvard was trying to
keep from being scored upon.   In the football
chapter of his excellent book, *At the Sign of the
Dollar*, published in 1917 by Harper & Brothers,
Deland tells the rest of the story, as follows: —

When the first half was nearly finished without a
score, our left end was injured.   The best substitute
was sent in to take his place.   He was a seasoned player
who had been captain of the Harvard team in the previous season, and he had only one mania — that was to

beat Princeton, so I knew his spirit would be a riotous one. The ball was in Princeton's possession on Harvard's 24-yard line. I was waiting for the signal for play when Camp suddenly turned to me and said, "Watch this play closely; *it is going to be a touchdown for Princeton.*" Five seconds afterward the ball came back and a Princeton runner went through the Harvard line twenty-four yards for the prophesied score. In sheer amazement at his ability to call the critical play in advance, I turned to Camp for an explanation. He said it was perfectly simple. "I saw Princeton's quarterback looking at the substitute. That made me look at him. Your man was excited like one who, playing on the end of the line, would defy caution, rush headlong into the defense, and overrun his man. As the Princeton quarterback never took his eyes off your man, I suspected that the play was going against him. It was a sure enough opening. The only question was, Did the Princeton quarter see it? Well, he did."

In other words, Camp saw the nervously excited substitute, and he saw that the Princeton quarterback saw him. The play was a brilliant one; the quarterback who detected the weak spot gave a still more brilliant exhibition; but to my mind the man on the side lines who reasoned the whole thing out in a cold-blooded way gave the most brilliant exhibition of all.

Walter Camp gained leisure in the years after 1910. In business, as in football, he had passed out of the period of hard, nervous competition into the quieter work of an advisor. His duties, both in sport and in business, did not become easier, but they took less time, and left him free for a number of minor avocations.   He wrote a manual of bridge whist, and did other desultory work of no great importance.   His days of long business application were nearly over.   It had been an interestingly continuous career, very unlike that of men who are wooed by impatience away from one job and into another.   In 1883 he joined the sales force of the Manhattan Watch Company in New York City, leaving it, after the only winter in his life he ever spent entirely out of New Haven, to enter the employ of the New Haven Clock Company.   These new employers sent him to New York again for a short time, after which he returned to its factory and main office in New Haven, where he was to remain uninterruptedly for more than forty years.   In 1886 he was made manager of the sales department; in January 1893 he was elected assistant treasurer.   He found the company's finances in a complicated position.   He was mature and experienced enough to attack this problem with deliberation.   As one of his associates says of him, he was not spectacular in his methods, "but could inspect any situation, from the lie of a golf ball to the future movement of the interest rate on money, without noticing elements which had no special importance, no matter how these might intrude on him."

Camp knew which of his own prejudices would

clarify and which would help his judgment. He was a very careful man. He was not an impetuous, lightning-swift driver of other men. He disliked to make quick decisions. In fact, he was probably unable by nature to arrive at conclusions with a bound. Some successful business executives have a strange faculty of coming all at once to a decision, and they find in a remarkably large number of instances that the quick decision was the right one. Camp, by contrast, was a plodder. He not only was unable to reach the right decision quickly, but was unable to reach any decision quickly. He hated all emergencies which required an abrupt opinion. He possessed unusual foresight, which made such emergencies unlikely to occur. Just as he tried in football to be "a jump ahead of the other fellow," so he tried in business to keep ahead of events. When he could foresee events, as he was likely to do on account of his freedom from distractions, he did not hesitate to shape a plan. He had, moreover, great tenacity of faith, based on confidence in his own judgment. This enabled him to hold firmly to a charted course, in spite of seeming discouragements. He believed that a sound policy would remain a sound policy, even though threatened by difficulties arising after its adoption. These qualities invested him with a business judgment that was more than merely shrewd. Walter Camp was canny.

I realize, as I write these words, that they do

not present a lively picture of a business career.
Camp's business career was not lively.   It cannot
be made to seem so.   He did not have, in forty
years, as many vicissitudes and adventures in business as James J. Hill, for instance, or as Edward
H. Harriman often crowded into forty days.   He
was inferior to them in business ambition.   He did
not like the kind of business adventures that made
them famous.   But he chose his own career wisely,
knowing his own limitations.

By 1902 he had become treasurer and general
manager of the New Haven Clock Company, and
a year later he was elected president.   He never
felt much interest in the factory, devoting himself to the financial and selling side of the business.
Edwin P. Root, who had emerged into prominence from the manufacturing division of the company at the time when Camp was winning his
way forward among its salesmen, took over the
burdens of the manufacturing department.   Later
he became president of the company, while Camp
took up what was to him more congenial advisory
work as chairman of the board of directors.
Camp had one attribute which most men lack,
and which Root appraised at its full value.   "Walter Camp was a nationally known man," he said.
"In any situation where a difficult piece of nego-
tiation was necessary, Camp's prominence made
him invaluable.   Any man in America was flat-
tered to meet him.   He could represent us before

any committee, or at any meeting, and do us
unusual credit."

The business career which Camp mapped out
for himself was not an exciting one, but it was the
right career for a man who had an absorbing
special interest outside of business.   It brought him
a snug fortune.   Only a few months before his sudden death, he said to his wife : "Whatever happens
to me, Alice, you will be comfortable.   We 've
saved two hundred and fifty thousand dollars."
Then, with a burst of his instinctive generosity,
he added : "*You* did it, Alice !"   When his estate
was appraised, the sum proved to be much larger
than he had said.   And Mrs. Camp had not known,
or sought to know, how much he was making at
any time.   This was the unusual kind of family
who know how to control their expenses, even
while their income is increasing.   They were never
in that spendthrift class which lives comfortably
at first on thirty dollars a week, and then becomes
poor on thirty thousand dollars a year.

Walter Camp found in the New Haven Clock
Company a sufficiently wide field for all the business success he cared about.   He was not tied to
his desk, like so many business men, but could
get away often for an afternoon or a week.   He
was not among the men who pretend to despise
business success, but he would have been sorely
pained in spirit if he had not become the leading
man in his company, or had found himself lacking

the comforts which he had known as a boy. His
father, Leverett L. Camp, was a school-teacher,
and could not earn much money; but he owned
a good deal of property in New Britain and Meri-
den. The family lived in a large and comfortable
house, with a summer home on Martha's Vineyard,
and their son was given nearly everything that he
expressed a desire for. Life was simpler then, of
course, and boys did not have extravagant desires.
Walter Camp's mother was a woman of unusual
refinement. Her son inherited from her his high
ideals and his love of poetry. She always had at
least one servant, and when she baked one of the
chocolate cakes which the men who came to the
house when they were boys still remember, she
did so because she enjoyed their appreciation, and
not because she was forced to do her own work.

Toward the end of his life, Walter Camp's
father lost his money, and Camp was obliged to
make his own way. He had therefore more respect for money than if he had merely inherited it.
He pursued the old and unbeatable plan of earn-
ing a little more than he spent, and of investing
the surplus wisely. He was ready at all times to
take advice from those early friends who had become leading figures in finance.

The years before the war found him busy with
a variety of interests, but he was not particularly
satisfied. *Collier's Weekly* had dropped the "Outdoor America" department which had interested

Camp for a long time. Once, indeed, he had been asked to take a leading part in the administration and editing of that side of the weekly, but his other interests had prevented his acceptance. He found that there is little advantage in contributing, at long range, to a magazine, especially when one's contributions take the form of editorial comment on events that are cold before the paragraphs are published. Camp enjoyed writing in his library after dinner, but the journalistic side of his life had worn thin. It was to be revived later in the form of regular and successful work for a newspaper syndicate; but there was a time when Camp felt the dejection and sense of futility that comes to all writers. There was no real outlet, for a while, for his strong vitality. Yale no longer wanted him as a football coach. Business success had come, and no longer absorbed his real interest. He had a very genuine horror of slipping into a rather lazy old age. Yet he did not feel old. He was beginning to earn regular dividends on the fund of physical strength which he had been laying up for himself.

It is even true that he felt a certain hard-to-define, vague impatience with the football men with whom he had worked so long. It would be absurd to say that he ever grew bored, for one moment, with football itself. But there are some letters of his to William H. Langford that may be quoted in this place. In one of them he wrote: —

My patience has been strained almost to the breaking point, for many years, with quarrels of all kinds, and my only reason for burdening you with them is your good nature, and also the fact that I believe we ought to have more brains on the job.

In another letter, this paragraph shows Camp's sense of the burden he had been carrying : —

I want to thank you for your coöperation, and all the work you have done in these answers to queries.   This has indeed been a great help to all of us.   It was bad enough in the twenty years when I was doing it alone, but I do think that this year the queries have shown a little more sense, and that speaks well for the improvement of understanding.

And a little later we find him writing : —

I should have written you earlier, telling you how much I appreciated your coming up that night so that we might go over the rules.   It would have been so easy for you not to do it, and it was such a great help to me, that I must write and say what a brick you are on all occasions and under all conditions.

These are the letters of a man somewhat troubled in spirit.   He was like an old knight hovering, a little wistfully, on the edge of the tourney field. There was no doubt, in the minds of his friends, that he missed the old thrill of accomplishment, the old and happy days when, like Ulysses, — whom in more ways than one he resembled, — he had been accustomed "to drink delight of battle with his peers."

But then came a sound, literally, of trumpets; and he found himself riding back into the field.

The war brought a new set of personal problems into every man's life. At the outset, the war gave Walter Camp a chance for renewed business activity. He enjoyed this new draft on his energy. Foreign orders came in, and could not be filled for lack of cargo space. Camp was greatly interested in finding ways not only of selling clocks but of packing them — of packing more of them, for instance, into a hundred cubic feet of space than had ever been packed before. There was a sudden shortage of materials and labor, affording new problems to be solved. Then, with the entry of America into the war, all business considerations left Camp's mind. Men of his age were showing their characters, now, more than they had ever shown them. Some were hurrying to Washington; others were staying sulkily at home, wondering why Washington did not send for them. Many were going to recruiting offices. A few were hiding from the call to duty. Others were guessing correctly that the one great chance in all their lives to make money easily had come. The whole structure of men's lives was changing. Walter Camp made no rapid decision. The call, when it came to him, was one that he did not expect. It took the form of a letter from a naval officer, complaining of the system of physical exercise prescribed for recruits, and asking Camp if he could suggest something better.

A little investigation at the naval training stations persuaded Camp that this criticism was well founded. He found that his correspondent had been right in saying that the old-fashioned setting-up drill exhausted the men who followed it faithfully, while the men who wished to take it lightly were able to go through the motions without doing any real work. "I had casually examined the various forms of Swedish setting-up drills before this time," wrote Camp, "but I had not realized that they strongly invite staleness and over-training."

For several weeks Camp watched the incoming recruits, and he paid attention, too, to the men who were rejected. Never before had he seen so many boys in need of physical training. He was horrified by the prevalence of flat feet; of other mechanical defects in the bones and joints of the hands and feet; of tuberculosis; and of other preventable troubles. Surgeon-General Ireland was to publish, after the war, the statistics which showed that of the 2,753,922 men examined for service, 1,320,934, or 48 per cent, were rejected as unfit. "This," said Camp, "is the most damning arraignment of a great country that has ever been published. I could believe that some such result would have been found in an examination of older men.   But these were boys and young men, the flower of our young manhood.   What kind of attention have we given them at school?   What kind of ignorance must have existed in their homes?   In the hour of need we found that nearly half of them had been too badly fed and too badly shod, or were too full of preventable disease, to be able to lead the simple outdoor life of a soldier in camp."

But it was not with the unfit men that Camp was to deal at this moment.   He put on a uniform, and began to labor with those who were fit. He was struck by their lack of resistance to disease.

At the first station I visited, [he wrote] the hospital was a pest house.   Lads were in bed with sharp attacks of measles, or sitting around in the throes of mumps, chicken pox, and other children's diseases.   Their bodies offered little resistance to the bacteria that carried these minor plagues; and they were in equally poor condition to resist serious contagions like meningitis, scarlet fever, and influenza.   The surgeons were keenly alert to prevent the spread of such diseases, but their efforts were largely negatived by the overtiring effect of the setting-up drill.   My task was to devise a simple system of movements that would build resistance — not crush it.   That was why I worked out the Daily Dozen.

Twelve simple movements were found to meet the needs, so the young men would resist fatigue as well as contagion.   Having worked out these movements, I tried them on classes of men, emphasizing that they

were to be done lightly and naturally, more in the spirit
of refreshment than with lips compressed, lungs heaving,
and muscles tightly flexed.

It is a curious thing that Walter Camp should
have been fifty-eight years old when this work engaged his attention.   There are countries in which
he would have been invited into public service
long before a war came along.   But he was faced by
the strange American indifference to health, so
remarkable in a nation that is deeply interested
in cures for disease.   Preventive measures of all
kinds have been unpopular in America.   There is
widespread love of patent medicines, to be taken
after the symptoms show themselves; but there is
no national fondness for fresh air in sleeping-rooms,
for inoculation in any form, or for regular exercise.   Camp had been thrown, all his life, with
young athletes from among the upper class — men
to whom the use of the toothbrush, for instance,
is as natural as breakfast itself.   Now, for the first
time, Camp met the common man in large num-
bers: the flat-footed, ill-nourished, unequally developed man, who takes no interest in hygiene.
Walter Camp expected to find strong, vigorous
boys who needed only a little hardening.   He
remarked after a few weeks of experience that it
was torture to him to watch the average boy strip
for physical examination.   Camp himself had perfect digestion; he had a taut, springy, muscular

coat of armor all over him. He never caught cold, or suffered from headaches and bilious attacks. He walked like an Indian, with his feet straight and a fine swinging roll of his leg from the hip. His chest was deep. He sat and stood bolt upright — the kind of man who resists fatigue and illness, who can keep going indefinitely.

Having taught the Daily Dozen to the physical instructors at the naval training stations, Camp went by request to Washington. No man went there during the war on a more important mission. It was up to him to find a way of keeping the highest government officials from breaking down under the strain of the war. Men had cracked in Great Britain and France. The history of the war will never be written in terms of the health of the men who directed it, but it might well be. And so might the history of the years of the peace which have followed.

However, it was a piece of good fortune for the men who sent for Camp that they did not send for any one of a dozen other men, — proprietors of health farms and institutes. For Camp merely announced that a voluntary morning class would meet at 7 : 30 A.M. behind the Treasury Building. The Cabinet attended this class. They came to the first meeting with visions of back-breaking setting-up drill. Camp merely had them take off their coats and run through the Daily Dozen once, and lightly. Therefore they came again. They expected dietary rules, but Camp suggested none. He advised a bath and rubdown before breakfast, nothing more. It was a light régime, but it succeeded. Not a man in that class broke down until the war ended, and many of them continued to do the Daily Dozen after the strain was gone.

It is a pity, perhaps, that the Daily Dozen was not made part of the official regulations of the Army and Navy. For it is safe to say that not many discharged soldiers have seen the slightest reason for keeping up the hard, tedious, setting-up drill which they were taught.

But Camp came out of the war with a great vision of new and greater public usefulness for himself. He saw that the Daily Dozen had possibilities for greater usefulness than he had supposed when he devised it. He wondered how to exploit it. There were a few days when he thought seriously of accepting an offer from men who wanted to establish a Walter Camp Health Institute, with himself at its head. But he put this invitation by. He was not a doctor, and he had no ambition to become a Muldoon. He knew well, after reflection, that the proposed institute would not attract young men who wanted to keep fit, but would become a refuge for elderly wrecks who wanted to recover from excesses of all kinds. He contented himself by writing a magazine article about the Daily Dozen. This article had sudden, unexpected results.

VIII

THE DAILY DOZEN

THE great-hearted nature of Walter Camp — the quality that used to be called magnanimity — proved itself when he gave away the Daily Dozen, with no thought of personal gain. It was the same quality that he had shown so often in his football career, as player and coach. For instance, there was a fine example of it after the Yale–Princeton game in 1911.

Rain had fallen all through the night, and the field was sodden and soft. The most dangerous man on the Princeton team was Sam White, an end who had won the Princeton–Harvard game by making a long run after a Harvard try for a field goal had been blocked. But the whole Princeton team that year was formidable; it was one of those teams for which everything seems to go right. In its game against Dartmouth, earlier in the season, a try for goal fell short, bounded erratically, and then hopped over the crossbar. This contingency was not provided for in the rules, and Walter Camp and his associates were forced to legislate against it after that season.

When Yale faced Princeton, on a sodden and soft field, White's ability to follow the ball showed itself almost at once. He picked up a fumbled ball near the Princeton goal line, and raced down the field with it. Close behind him ran Langford, the referee. From behind, in a slightly quartering direction, came Arthur Howe, Yale's quarterback and captain. These three sped toward the Yale goal, with Howe gaining. On the five-yard line he dived at White from the rear. The Princeton man tumbled. Rolling over and over, he slid and stumbled the last few yards for a touchdown.

It was up to Langford to decide whether the touchdown was legal or not. If Howe had caught White in his grasp, the ball was "dead" at the point where the tackle had been made. But Langford ruled that Howe had not tackled White, but had merely upset him by striking his heel with his shoulder. The touchdown was therefore allowed, and it won the game. A little later, a photograph was brought out which seemed to show Howe's arm encircling White's legs. When Langford was shown this photograph, he maintained that the decision had been right — that White had not been tackled and stopped. Camp's comment was brief: —

"You were right, Bill. Picture or no picture, you saw what happened."

It was a game that he specially hoped Yale might win, for Walter Camp, Jr., was playing at halfback, where Walter Camp had played so many years before. But Camp could be trusted to accept decisions in the spirit of a chivalrous gentleman who plays for the sake of the game, and who watches it in the same spirit. The decisions in football often take victory away from one side and give it to the other. It is to the enduring credit of Langford and of a hundred other fair and sportsmanlike officials that these decisions in the big games are accepted with good grace by everyone. Camp himself had shown the way when, as referee of the Yale–Princeton game in 1885, he had ruled that Beecher of Yale had stepped out of bounds during a long run for a touchdown, and that Lamar of Princeton had not.

He was now to show the same generous spirit in giving away his Daily Dozen exercises. Everyone knows that the American public will buy almost any desirable novelty in mind- or body-building if it is presented in the form of a "course." For instance, there was a very profitable course in memory-training, well advertised by the mention of an imaginary incident concerning Mr. Addison Sims of Seattle. There are other courses, ranging in subject from executive business management to the collection and sale of butterflies. There are dozens of "health courses" and "body-building courses." Walter Camp had material for one of these profitable courses, and he knew he had it. Advertised in flamboyant style, and backed by hundreds of testimonials from the most prominent men in America, the Daily Dozen could have been sold profitably for many years.

But Camp was not a man to make extravagant claims for the Daily Dozen, nor did he wish to trade upon public credulity. "I have never made any money except by my business, my investments, and my books," he said. "If the Daily Dozen were really pushed commercially, it would make a fortune. But I know it will help people in private as much as it helped the naval recruits and the men in Washington, and I don't want to appear to be one of those woolly-headed physical culturists. I would rather give it away."

He accepted without hesitation an invitation from John M. Siddall, editor of the *American Magazine*, to present the Daily Dozen in its pages. By so doing, he virtually destroyed his own ownership of the Daily Dozen, for the twelve movements were now available to more than a million people. Camp received a moderate check, at regular rates, from this magazine; it was but a tiny fraction of what he would have made by selling the Daily Dozen as a physical culture course. But he was in the spirit of wartime service. He was shocked by the run-down condition of so many young men. He was delighted to receive, instead of money, thousands of letters from people who heard about the Daily Dozen and invited him to come and demonstrate it in their homes, their business offices, and their clubs. He had, however, virtually destroyed his own copyright in the Daily Dozen.

Then he went to the office of *Collier's Weekly*,

which had shortly before that time become affil-
iated with the Crowell Publishing Company,
owners of the *American Magazine* and *Woman's
Home Companion*.

"I want to present the Daily Dozen more fully,"
he said. "Perhaps I can answer some of the
questions that are coming to me about it."

He had put aside two temptations to exploit it
commercially, and he was not impressed by the
fact that Eugen Sandow and Lieutenant Müller
were reputed to have made a great deal of money
out of systems of exercise.

"They have made only a cent or two out of each
thousand dollars that has been made, and will still
be made, out of physical culture," he replied.
"People are greedy for it, and can't get enough of
it. Promise a boy that you can teach him to chin
himself with one hand, and he will pay you for lessons. Promise a middle-aged man or woman that
you can melt fat away without too much pain,
and you can keep them coming to you for months.
The private gymnasium is a gold mine. I expect
to see a large industry, presided over by ex-trainers
of prizefighters and woolly-headed physical culture 'professors' of one kind and another. But
I won't let myself into it. My wife has an entirely
proper horror of it. Any attempt on my part to
make money out of the Daily Dozen would be
regarded as an effort to capitalize my reputation
in amateur athletics."

What Camp said at that time about the success of commercial physical culture has come abundantly true, as anyone can find out by studying the advertising pages of the cheaper magazines, and noting the many opportunities offered to develop strength and beauty at home. Each of the large cities has many private gymnasiums for the deflated business man and his inflated wife.

Camp had lectured informally on the Daily Dozen, and was seriously taxing his strength by traveling from one city to another, giving talks and lessons, now to a group of bank directors and officers on the roof of a great city bank, now to the executives of a manufacturing company in the noon hour. He thought he could satisfy many of these requests by a complete article, or series of articles, in which he would not only describe the Daily Dozen, but give his whole philosophy of health.

As a writer, he was not a man who cared to have anything printed until it was as good as it could be made. So much of my own life has been spent among people who are crazy to fly into print that I always enjoyed working with this man, to whom careful preparation was a fetish. Camp was not among those small-minded people who object to corrections made in their manuscript by competent copy-readers. He agreed cheerfully to cuts whenever they speeded up his story, just as he was grateful for other editorial changes made for the sake of clarity or of completeness. An editor cherishes such authors, even as he dislikes the other kind. Camp returned to New Haven. After a while he wrote that he had done the ground-work of his proposed Daily Dozen article, and asked for a competent writing man as collaborator.

Every writer will know what he was up against. It is easy enough to describe the Daily Dozen accurately, and to make some commonplace re-marks about it. It would have been still easier to praise it gaudily as a cure for most diseases, including old age. Camp did neither of these things. He sat down and asked himself how he could make people realize that they needed the Daily Dozen, even though they might be sure they did not want it. He knew that calisthenics are not popular. He felt that he would have to jounce people out of a false security. " Too many men," he wrote, " think that they have done their duty by ' taking ' exercise or ' taking ' medicine. A man who belongs to a country club fancies that he leads a country life. There is no value, except amusement, change of scene, in that kind of exer-cise. Week-end golf and tennis are nothing but amusements. We must make people know that they have internal muscles, and know why these muscles must be kept elastic. Mineral oil won't do it. The Daily Dozen will."

He thought of the men he knew whose stomachs were many inches larger around than their chests.

He thought of the sallow women who never feel really well. He knew it was useless to tell them to go back to nature and lead healthy outdoor lives. He searched for some creature that has learned to adapt itself to the same kind of life. He found such a creature at the fireside — the common domestic cat.

He wrote about the cat's ability to keep well, based on the curious, instinctive, stretching exercises which the cat is always performing. Then he switched to the tiger. The tiger is so big that you must notice it, and the tiger manages to keep well and live a long time, even when locked in a cage. Why? Camp went to the Zoo, and found the tiger endlessly stretching itself. He made inquiries, and satisfied himself that the tiger knew something that the civilized man and woman do not know. Then he gave the answer, and the answer made the Daily Dozen a household word. "Take a tip from the tiger and keep young," he wrote. "Live faster, but don't die faster." He was always a phrase-maker of great skill. He had a gift of expressing an idea in few words. He knew the value of alliteration: All-America — Daily Dozen — Take a Tip from the Tiger. And it was in such short, easily remembered sentences that he proposed to tell what he knew about health. The very names of the movements in the Daily Dozen sing themselves into your memory. Grate, Grind, Grasp. Curve, Crawl, Curl. But there were many complicated ideas to be put into his exposition. He knew the heart, for instance, can become infiltrated with fat, and that if you slough off this fat too quickly you may injure the heart, which has grown used, as it were, to the soft bed-clothes in which it is wrapped. He believed that the Daily Dozen, by replacing the normal activi-ties of aboriginal man, could either take fat off a heavy body or put it on a lean one. He saw in it, not a cure for inactivity of the intestinal muscles, but a way in which to develop those muscles. He knew from his personal experience, and from a remarkable encounter that he once had with an apparently crazy man in a sleeping car, that the Daily Dozen is an admirable preventive of insom-nia. On that occasion, a conductor had come through the car in a state of great anxiety.

"Are you a doctor?" he asked.

"Almost," replied Camp.

"There is a man on this train who says he has n't been able to sleep for many nights," explained the conductor. "I think he has gone crazy. Can you give him an injection or something that will put him to sleep?"

"Try for a doctor," answered Camp. "If there is none on the train, I will see what I can do."

He took the sufferer to the baggage car, and put him through the Daily Dozen. Its physiological or mental effect became apparent at once. The man accepted Camp's calm statement that he would now go to sleep. He did go to sleep, and he remained permanently grateful to the man who had shown him the way.

Camp's collaborator, in working out his careful exposition of the Daily Dozen, was William Almon Wolff, a former college athlete who had let himself grow too heavy, while his muscles grew soft. Camp and Wolff wrote and polished the manuscript, and Camp incidentally put Wolff through the Daily Dozen, until he grew so supple that he posed for the illustrations of the twelve movements. Wolff returned from New Haven with the article. It appeared in *Collier's Weekly*, dated August 5, 1920; and, for the first and last time in my experience, a single article sold out the entire edition of a large national magazine. Not a copy could be found for love or money. A reprint had to be made of the article, to satisfy thousands of inquirers.

Camp had accepted his regular author's rate for this extraordinary article, but refused to take more for it. Finally a ten-cent pamphlet was printed, with a modest royalty for Walter Camp which, after some hesitation, he agreed to accept. More than four hundred thousand copies were sold. Then another company asked permission to put the Daily Dozen into the form of phonograph records, with results that must be known to nearly every owner of a phonograph.

Near the end of his life, with the Daily Dozen

selling like wildfire in pamphlet form, and also in phonograph records and in moving pictures, Walter Camp wrote a little book about it, which was published by the Reynolds Publishing Company, of New York. This was his last book, and he put into it a great deal of his philosophy of work and life. The introduction is by Dr. Samuel W. Lambert, most eminent of American heart specialists. He wrote: —

This book is Camp's final word to his many followers. He preaches from beginning to end one chief lesson — moderation. He advises a routine for the year, about as follows: 295 working days, with three weeks' regular vacation, and 49 Sundays for rest from regular business duties. In addition, he prescribes ten hours of outdoor play a week, and the Daily Dozen once a day, seven days in the week. Such a routine should keep the people of this country in better health than they now enjoy. . . . Camp has promised much for this system of routine exercise if it be properly done, nor has he promised too much. He has added other rules than the regular performance of the Daily Dozen: he warns against excesses of every kind, of overeating, of overdrinking and of oversmoking. He knows that there is no absolute rule applicable to everyone. He is no teetotaller, but a thorough advocate of true temperance. His promise to remove insomnia and a sluggish digestion from the world, to reduce fat, and to add to the gracefulness of the human race, form an ideal in which he thoroughly believed, and which will come the nearer to accomplishment by a wider adoption of his rules for a middle path of moderation in all things which make up the routine of life. . . . One may differ from Camp in some of his minor conclusions, but no physician and no athlete can object to his rules for moderation in eating and in drinking and in exercise. No one can doubt that the carrying out of these rules in a natural way will help any individual to do better, harder, and more continuous brain work, and that the Daily Dozen will bring to anyone suppleness, if not growth; endurance, if not strength; tone, if not new power. It will give to anyone cleaner outlines and fat-free muscles.

To such a recommendation of Camp's programme for public health it is hardly necessary to add the individual letters that came to him. He was not a doctor, but he had grateful patients everywhere. Letters came to him from Connecticut and from China. A middle-aged man in Waterbury amazed himself, after trying the Daily Dozen for a while, by pitching seven innings against a team of high-school boys. General Charles H. Sherrill, who in his college days won seven intercollegiate track championships, wrote to Camp that he did the Daily Dozen for a month, and then emerged without one sore spot from a hard squash match with his boy. Another old friend, cheerfully introducing himself as an enemy, reported that the Daily Dozen had brought him down from 210 to 188 pounds. Amid a chorus of remarks like, "You are a benefactor," and "I want to cure a sick man, just as you cured me,"

Camp felt that the million readers of *Collier's Weekly* and the four hundred thousand readers of the pamphlet were really taking a long stride back to youth and strength. And this was before the phonograph and the radio had extended the work. It was fitting that in the long run he should have made some money out of the Daily Dozen, for at the time when its commercial exploitation was open to him, he pushed the prospective money away with both hands.

He was himself the best possible walking advertisement of what genuine physical culture can do. His coolness on a hot day was always conspicuous. I once went to New Haven on a blistering hot August morning, hailed by the newspapers as the hottest day in many years. Camp was sitting in coat and waistcoat in his office, as cool as the proverbial cucumber. He would loll in a deep easy-chair, and then spring forward and upward out of it with no telltale push on the arms. (This, by the way, is one of the two tests of old age. The other is a little more intricate. Drop something on the floor, and see if you instinctively snatch it up with a sideways bend of your body, like a child, or if you have to get squarely in front of it and hoist your weight up and down in a straight line. Camp invented these two tests, and delighted in applying them, without warning or comment, to everyone.) He was like rubber and steel, himself. He never showed fatigue; his head and shoulders never drooped forward. His shoulder blades met each other in the middle of his flat back. He carried his head up and his chin in, but there was no ramrod stiffness in his bearing. He could sit — and this is a great test of physical fitness — for many hours at a meeting with no twisting of his hands or writhing in his chair. Asked how he accomplished this unusual feat of sitting still, he gave this rather remarkable piece of advice: "All business conferences are physically tiresome. The best man alive, mentally, cannot sit through them quietly and keep his mind on business, unless he stretches his arms and legs beforehand. I go over to the washroom and put myself through the Daily Dozen. Try it before you face your next long conference, and see if it will not help you to keep more alert."

He was a smoker who smoked very little, and a drinker who drank a practically irreducible minimum. He took more exercise than enough to counteract any possible bad effect of either habit. He was interested in long life — or more accurately, in long youth. Impressed by Mark Twain's remark that human life is arranged wrong-side-foremost, and that we really ought to live backward and have youth as a reward, he found himself presenting the Daily Dozen more and more as a sort of fountain of youth. He scorned the man who grows middle-aged at forty and really old at sixty. He said biting things about such men, things that brought out the dour streak in his character, the vein of caustic which he usually repressed.   He had no respect for any father or husband who neglected the ordinary and simple rules of health.   No one who knew Walter Camp ever called him a prig.   He knew many men who did not lead straight lives.   But he was less contemptuous, in private conversation, of a man who hurt himself as the result of real physical temptation than of the man who simply let his good boyish body go to seed in early middle life.   He had a great scorn for the semi-drunkard, and for the man who lights one cigarette from the butt of another.

"Take the habit of smoking too much," he said. "It's just a habit; you enjoy tobacco much more if you use it sparingly.   We know that smoking is bad for young people, in any amount.   It is apparently harmless to many older people, if not indulged to excess.   That is all we can say positively.   But Nature has a way of saying the same thing with true emphasis.   Take the man who smokes too much.   He wakes some night with an agonizing pain — a pain under his left breast, a pain that stops his breath.   He writhes all night, or else screams for help.   The doctor comes, takes his blood pressure, listens to his heart, and tells him to quit smoking except for a pipe or two after meals. What happens?   Nature cashes his check for this first overdraft.   The man's heart steadies itself; his blood pressure goes down.   He feels so well, after a while, that he starts smoking like a chimney again. And then? No man can fool Nature. She comes to his bedside another night and says: "You could n't learn, could you? You have had your chance. I 've better men than you. Time 's up."

With his dark eyes blazing, and his voice sinking to the same rasp that he had once used to impress some stupid player on the football field, Walter Camp could deliver this little parable in a way that made it unforgettable.

More and more he came to the opinion that a healthy body begets a healthy mind, and that the first duty of a nation is to train its young men to resist strain and fatigue. "The dominant nation of the future," he said, "will be the one that can send most men to the top of the Matterhorn."

The doctor in Walter Camp came to the surface of his life again in these closing years. This man, who had once confessed that he could not stand the sight of blood, was a born healer. He remarked that calisthenics are unpopular, by their very nature, and that the man or woman who did the Daily Dozen regularly, year after year, would be an exception. He knew that it would add one more duty to a day already crowded with duties. He advised people to subtract that fifteen minutes from the business day. "If you can't do the Daily Dozen and catch your regular 8 : 07 o'clock train," he said, "I would advise you to do it anyway, and catch a later train. If it makes you fifteen minutes late at the office, you will nevertheless have the cheering knowledge that it may make you fifteen years later at the cemetery."

He became, at the same time, very much interested in diet. In his early days he urged the use of vegetables, insisting on moderation in the amount of food consumed and making the suggestion — altogether opposed to the old English athletic training regimen — that water is a sufficiently satisfying drink. In later life Camp devoured books on dietary methods, although he did not devour the nuts, zwiebach, fermented milk, and other fads urged by their authors. He wrote many articles against fads and superstitions in diet. He found himself writing with zest. A campaign he waged single-handed for cheaper golf — after discovering that the annual dues at a golf club like Hoylake in England cost less than a single average round of golf at an American country club — brought him many letters from young professional men who found golf too expensive, and also promoted the building of many municipal courses.

But it was with boys and children that Camp found himself in most sympathy as he passed sixty years. Any request from them was sure of careful and generous action on his part. He became a grandfather in 1917, and hoped to see Walter Camp III grow up to take his place as a Yale halfback, in the position where two generations of Walter

Camps had played. To this boy and his mother, Frances English Camp, Walter Camp was a perpetual source of delight. He had, in Victor Hugo's phrase, "the art of being a grandfather." And he was equally kind to all other boys. The young son of his friend John T. Doyle, president of the American Sports Publishing Company, asked him to write an article for a school magazine published by the Brainard School for Boys. Young Jack Mercier Doyle did not know, perhaps, that Camp was one of the three or four most highly paid writers of non-fiction in America. But Camp sat down at once and wrote a short, clear essay on one great change in the modern game. It is worth reprinting here : —

The Development of Modern American Football

The simplest way to show how radically the sport of American football has altered since its original introduction into this country is to describe the progress of interference, for it is upon this feature that the game shows its extreme departure from the parent stem of Rugby football.

In the strict Rugby Union rules, as adopted in 1876, in this country, any man once ahead of the ball (that is, between the ball and his opponents' goal) was not only offside but could no longer take part in the play or interfere in any way with his opponents. As soon, therefore, as Americans tried to play the game they found great difficulty. When the ball was "heeled out," or dragged back with the foot, according to the rules, all the rush line must, theoretically, melt into thin air.

This was manifestly impossible, and rush-line players not only refused to disappear but began quite earnestly to take part in the play. The first step toward interference was taken when these rushers extended their arms horizontally from their sides and thus formed a bulwark in front of their runners, which quite effectually prevented the opposing would-be tacklers from breaking through the line.

It was not long before they went still further, and actually wrapped their arms about their opponents. This naturally and speedily led to a crisis in the game, for it made defense impossible; so it became necessary to decide whether to eliminate by very strict rules all interference, or offside play, or else draw a line somewhere up to which interference with the defense would be legal, beyond which it must not go.

This took on the form of a rule whose principles still govern interference in the modern game. It was this: A side in possession of the ball shall be permitted to make use of their bodies in any way they like, to interfere with the progress of their opponents, but cannot, under penalty of a foul, use their hands and arms in any way to accomplish this purpose. On the other hand, the defenders can make use of their hands and arms in an endeavor to break through and get at the runner. Thus, theoretically, the principle was established that the side not in possession of the ball had the right of way or the greater privilege bestowed by permitting them to thus use their hands and arms, while such action was forbidden to the side in possession.

This method has prevailed through the history of the progress of the sport in this country and upon its principle has been built up the great structure of attack and defense, which has made the modern American game such a scientific possibility with all its complicated system of signals and attack, well balanced by a defense that must be planned and thought out with equal care.

Any boy, anywhere, who asked Walter Camp for help received it, in full measure. The boys at Lawrenceville School asked him at one time to come over and show them why they were not just then playing winning football. Camp made the journey, and labored with the team for some time before his presence was known to the head master. The football coach at Groton School, who had known Camp only casually, invited him on another occasion to come for a visit. Camp responded, arrived on the field during practice, and asked to see the plays which the Groton team had been taught.

"Your plays are sound and simple," he said, "but you are up against a strong St. Mark's team that may keep you from scoring. What you really need is a more elaborate play, that might give you a touchdown toward the end of the game."

He developed, then and there, a play that was altogether novel in schoolboy football at the time; a play based on an extremely wide "spread" formation. The boys practised it, and were enthusi-

astic.   They wanted to use it at the very beginning
of the game.

"If you do that, it won't work," said Camp.
"You must wait till the St. Mark's ends are tired,
and a little careless.   Use the play as near the end
of the game as you dare, and it may go for a touchdown."

His advice was taken too literally.   In desperate
need of a touchdown to save the game, the Groton
coach sent in a substitute in the last minute of play
with instructions to the quarterback to try Walter
Camp's play.   Groton had the ball in her own
territory.   The play went for forty yards.   Lining
up quickly, the Groton quarterback signaled for
the same play again.   The St. Mark's ends were
tired, and the play resulted in a thirty-yard gain.
Then the whistle ended the game, before Groton
could carry the ball over for the saving touchdown.
But Walter Camp had given a lesson in strategy
which was remembered by the boys in seasons to
come.

The same fine, high spirit that Camp showed in
wanting to give the Daily Dozen away, thereby
refusing to capitalize his athletic reputation,
showed itself all the more brightly in all his inter-
course with boys.   In their eyes of course he had
additional glamor and prestige; he was "a star
of tournament," a man never excelled as player
and teacher of games.   It would have been easy
for him to sit down on this reputation, and show

himself aloof and unconcerned. There is a large class of college football coaches who work entirely for their own teams and their own security. But there is a small class who know that they hold a stewardship for the whole game. They know its effect on the minds of boys, and they are never more happy than when they are helping boys to play it, and to play it well. In this class was Walter Camp.

"One day Camp and I were picking plays for a school football team," wrote Lorin F. Deland, the Harvard coach. "I said: 'Why not give them the Butterworth dive?' He said: 'Do you think they could play it?' I replied: 'I could better express an opinion if I understood the play myself.' For two years it had been the one thing I wanted to understand before I died. And then Camp showed it to me. It was his adaptation in scrimmage form of my own principle of the previous year, the flying wedge. But it was twice as powerful, because the wedge was kept very sharp, and inside it was F. S. Butterworth, Yale's greatest hurdler. The play was practically built around him."

Even now, it is thrilling to think of these two famous football men sitting down together and "picking plays for a school team." And it was characteristic of Camp that, for the greater good of football, he let Deland know the working of a play that Deland could not fathom.

It was by a host of kindly acts of this kind that Walter Camp won not merely the respect of boys — for he had that already — but won their affection too. And boys were to remember their debt to him, after he died. The great Walter Camp Memorial at New Haven, finest of tributes to any athlete who ever lived, is being built in part by the voluntary, unsolicited contributions of school-boys throughout the country.

IX

THE WALTER CAMP MEMORIAL

On March 14, 1925, three men were sitting on the deck of a steamship in the Red Sea. They were all friends of Walter Camp; one of them indeed was almost his oldest friend. They talked of many things, and while they talked they took stock of one another, noticing the signs of premature old age which they all displayed, the unmistakable signs of life spent in offices, with not enough exercise, not enough of the moderation in all things which Walter Camp practised as well as preached.

"I wish," said one of them at last, "that all of us were as sure to live as long and keep as well as Walter Camp."

A steward came up, with a radiogram. Walter Camp was dead.

The news at this time was being published in newspapers everywhere. To everyone who knew Camp it came as a stunning surprise. For he was apparently in the full tide of health and vigor; he was within a month of his sixty-sixth birthday, but his step was as elastic, his eye as bright, and his bearing as full of muscular grace as at any time in the previous thirty years. He had no suspicion that his heart might fail, or he would have mentioned it to his family, and to that close friend of his who is the most eminent of heart specialists.   But Walter Camp had no reason to feel ill.   He went to the annual meeting of the Football Rules Committee on March 13, in New York.   He showed all his old zest at that meeting, although it was not one of the vitally important meetings of the kind which he had attended in so many earlier years.   The Committee had done its work.   There was no longer any storm of public disapproval to face.   It was not necessary for Camp to invent a radically new game, as he had done in 1883 by presenting his plan for the modern scrimmage, and for possession of the ball for three consecutive downs.   That rule abolished Rugby football in America, and launched the game into a new and uncharted sea.   He brought the centre and the quarterback into being at that time; just as he later debarred the graduate student from playing on college teams, and still later helped to banish mass plays and excessive injuries.   All these large reforms had been made.   It was therefore a meeting of only average importance to which he went. He carried his usual large collection of facts and notes upon which legislation could be based.   He had been on a long tour of the Western states, watching football everywhere.   In many places he had been given a reception that came as near being an ovation as his singularly modest spirit would permit.   And the meeting was a gathering

of his peers — such men as Edward K. Hall of
Dartmouth, William S. Langford of Trinity, Fred
W. Moore of Harvard, Alonzo A. Stagg of Chicago,
William W. Roper of Princeton, and the other
football men who signed the memorial resolution
which is quoted on a later page. But these men
did not come to the meeting to pass any such
resolution. Their business was merely to review
the past season in football and to pass any new,
minor rules that would benefit the game. They
knew that they would have Camp's guidance as
usual. He had been at all such meetings for
nearly fifty years, and he had given no sign that he
expected to withdraw. They had his guidance
for one day. He was the oldest man at the meeting, and the others remarked how well he was looking. He admitted, smilingly, that he was at work
on a book intended to show people how to keep
young and well at fifty, and afterward.

There can be no doubt that, in writing this book
on the Daily Dozen, Walter Camp regarded himself as an example of the truth of his teaching.
The book is aimed at the middle-aged reader.
It is one long plea for moderation, covering even
such tiny details as the unwisdom of pulling yourself up with your hands out of a swimming pool,
when you can more easily walk up the steps.
"You can live faster and not die faster," said
Walter Camp, urging his readers not to overtax
their strength. But he does not often mention

dying in this book — his thoughts are all about life, about more abundant and useful and happy living.

A little before midnight, the members of the committee said good-bye to Walter Camp. They did not know that they were saying good-bye, nor did he. They simply said "Good night." On the following morning, when he did not appear at the session, the door of his hotel room had to be forced, and it was found that he had died peacefully in his sleep. It was the sort of death that befitted him. As an apostle of health, he had never been ill. He felt none of the slow attack of old age; he was never to know the crippling, almost unmentionable little maladies that usually come, one after another, to men who have lived more than sixty years. His neck and throat had not fallen away, his well-cut clothes had not ceased to fit him, he was not forced to wear thin, flexible shoes. He was as lean and supple as ever — a man in superb physical condition. He was keeping up his golf. Only a few months before, he had mailed to the publisher of his Daily Dozen book one of his cards after a round at New Haven. That score happened to be 81 strokes; it was neither the best nor the worst of his last few rounds. His drives, never very long, were as long as ever; his approach shots and putts had all their old crispness and accuracy. He was still eating what he pleased. He had not had to make one physical readjustment of any kind.

And now, as the end came, he died on the scene, and in the very midst, of the activities that pleased him most. He was a man who kept his feelings under rigid control, and he was spared the agonies of farewells. He was the inventor and guardian of modern American football, and he died with football the last thought in his mind and with the full expectation of guiding its destinies on the morrow. And so he will, although he can attend no more meetings. Men die, but institutions continue. Walter Camp had lived to see football become an institution, and to put the impress of his chivalrous personality on the minds of the younger men who worked at his side.

Walter Camp was primarily a football legislator, and Percy D. Haughton was a coach. Both died in harness. In fact, Camp said that Haughton died a characteristic and happy death, stricken while in the very act of coaching a squad of players who looked up to him. It was Camp's fortune to die no less happily, with the football men whom he chiefly respected all around him, and with no cloud on the future of the game he loved. It can be truly said of him, as Owen Seaman said of Joseph Chamberlain, that "even death, last enemy of all, came to him like a friend."

Almost every newspaper in America paid full editorial tribute to Walter Camp as soon as the news of his death was known. But it is not in these tributes, fine as they were, that you will get the best measure of his importance and his character. The finest expressions came from the men who had worked with him. Take first of all the memorial resolution passed by the American Intercollegiate Football Rules Committee : —

His contribution to the game [it reads], covers a period of almost exactly half a century. It began at Yale in the fall of 1876, when he played in the first game of Rugby Football ever played by college teams in this country. It ended when he died in his sleep on the night of March 13–14, 1925, during an overnight intermission between sessions of the Rules Committee called together in New York City for the purpose of establishing the playing rules for the season of 1925.

From 1876 until 1910, when he retired from active participation in directing the strategy of Yale football, he was outstanding leader in the development of the playing technique and the strategy of the game.

From 1879 until 1925 he was a member of every football rules convention and every Rules Committee. During that period and literally up to the hour of his death he was the acknowledged leader in the evolution of the game through the framing of its playing rules.

In the deliberations of this Committee his counsel has been always wise and far-seeing, his attitude toward those with whose views he differed has been unfailingly generous and understanding, and his adherence to the highest standards of sportsmanship has been unwavering and inspiring.

It is in this last respect that Walter Camp made his greatest contribution to football. If football is to continue as the greatest of all academic sports, it will be due not alone to the foundations, toward the building of which Walter Camp contributed so generously, but in a far greater measure to the fine standards of American sportsmanship toward the establishment of which no man in America has contributed more, either by precept or by example.

American Rugby Football has lost its founder and its greatest champion, but his influence on the game will endure as long as the game is played.

E. K. Hall, Chairman

M. F. Ahearn	C. W. Savage
William S. Langford	H. J. Stegeman
Fred W. Moore	Dana X. Bible
William W. Roper	John J. McEwen
A. A. Stagg	C. Henry Smith
James A. Babbitt	George M. Varnell

There came, at this time, many thousands of letters to Mrs. Camp, and to Walter Camp, Jr. It is significant that while Yale men of all ages were fully represented, by no means all the letters came from them. Hundreds were from Princeton men who were old opponents of Camp's teams on the football field, and old friends of his at the same time. This is fully explained by the address made by Professor Charles W. Kennedy of Princeton at the Walter Camp Memorial Service held at Battell Chapel at Yale, on Monday of the 1925 Commencement Week at Yale. The address follows in part: —

Walter Camp was all his life a great and generous sportsman, hating flabbiness, and loving the hard, clean contest and the shining goal.   He recognized, as John Galsworthy has recognized, that in the troubled affairs of men sport has steadily kept a flag of idealism flying 'with its spirit of rules kept, and regard for the adversary, whether the fight is going for or against.' As a competitor, Walter Camp was endowed with a natural love of athletic games, and an ability to play them surpassingly well.   As an administrator of sports he displayed an unfailing shrewdness and invention in the formulation of wise rules and the development of sound and ingenious technique of play. As a sportsman, he strove with unswerving firmness throughout a long lifetime to infuse into the codes that govern sport a spirit of chivalry and magnanimity. As a citizen, he labored without ceasing to weave the love of athletic games into the fabric of our national life, in the faith that by this love and practice our boys may grow to stronger and finer manhood.

As one of the rule makers and elder statesmen of college athletics he was in unique degree responsible for the development of the game of football as it is known and played to-day from coast to coast.   It was the achievement of Walter Camp, almost single-handed, to evolve from the formless and hardly recognizable Rugby of the seventies the game' of modern American football — a game in which his unerring judgment and constructive vision infused a rapid thrust and parry, a balance of mass action and individual play, an intellectual ingenuity of attack and defense.   Through the long course of this evolution it was his influence, first and foremost, that shaped the destiny of the most popular of modern college games, and moulded it to an instrument for the testing of character and the training of manhood.

But many of us believe that America's debt to Walter Camp goes far beyond the things I have mentioned. His preëminence in the athletic world arose from the fact, though I never knew him to use the phrase, that he had a philosophy of sport. There was something almost Greek in his love of the lithe grace, the supple skill, the hard clean strength of the human body and in his admiration of those qualities of character that reveal themselves in the fine achievement of college sport. During the Great War, it was his all but immeasurable service, by the invention of his ingenious "Daily Dozen," to bring home to men by thousands and hundreds of thousands the joy of physical fitness.

When all is said the love that men have for sport, and the respect they hold for sportsmen, spring from an instinctive recognition that generous sportsmanship sows the seed of magnanimity — that from their playing fields our boys may carry to the work of life an ability to win greatly and to lose greatly.

Yale has the honor to claim him with pride as hers, but his friends were legion. His influence crossed all boundaries, drawing colleges closer in friendly competition, and joining sportsmen in a common devotion to the idealism of sport. The news of his death shadowed many a campus remote from New Haven. From Princeton, and from all lovers of college sport, I bring a memorial of affection and respect for a generous

opponent, a loyal friend, a sportsman without fear
and without reproach. His fame has no need of per-
petuating bronze. It will abide secure in the heart of
youth and in the memory of age.

An unforgettable picture of Walter Camp in his
daily life was presented at the same service by
Professor William Lyon Phelps of Yale, who closed
with a splendid and deserved tribute to Mrs.
Camp. Professor Phelps said : —

"Others have spoken to-day of Walter Camp as a
public man; I wish to say a few words about him as
my friend. About twenty-five years ago, we used to
go out to the Country Club nearly every day at noon,
and play eighteen holes together between twelve and
two o'clock. He knew that it was better for the average man, who had to be in his place of business both
morning and afternoon, to spend the midday interval
on the links rather than at the lunch table. But as
very few people seemed to share his opinion, Walter
and I practically had the course to ourselves. This
daily communion of two hours which it was my immense privilege to enjoy with him, gave the opportunity to talk about many things.

"I acquired an immense respect not merely for his
views on athletic contests, but for his opinions about
books, and about human nature. Walter was an excellent business man and an authority on all kinds of
outdoor and indoor sport. But he was exceedingly
well-read in general literature, and his criticisms of
new novels and essays, and of new plays at the theatre,

were original, well-founded, and penetrating. I have no doubt that had he chosen to specialize in any one of a half dozen fields of intellectual effort, he could have made a name for himself. But he wisely used his experience, his knowledge, and his capacity for leadership in teaching young America the highest ideals of sportsmanship during just the period when such teaching was most needed.

"Walter and I were often on the list of speakers at various alumni banquets; and I remember on one occasion, when a Yale graduate, who seemed to think there was something immoral about playing to win, made some sarcastic allusion to the overemphasis given to football, and attempted to reinforce his remarks by a quotation from Matthew Arnold, Walter, who spoke next, completed the quotation, and turned it successfully against his critic.

"In all the years I knew Walter Camp, and in all the conversations I had with him, I never heard him use bad language, I never heard him say anything querulous, petulant, or jealous. I never saw him overexcited, and I never heard him complain of the unfair treatment that had more than once been shown him. He was a man of the world, a gentleman always and everywhere, a splendid illustration of the ideals he preached.

"In the last ten or twelve years of his life, he was my neighbor; and as we both had the habit of early rising, I used to see him every morning about half-past seven on his way to business. In winter he carried his overcoat over his arm, and maintained a speed in walking as though he were out for a record. Like

all men in good physical condition, who love their business, who love recreation, who love their friends, and
who love life, he did not creep like a snail unwillingly
to work. He went to his office with the same joyful
eagerness that he went to the links. But he always
had time in these early mornings to stop for a moment
and talk. To see him and to speak with him freshened
me up for the whole day. He was so full of the very
abundance of life. There was something about him
so clean, so wholesome, so inspiring that I shall miss
his presence every day; but I shall be thankful always
that I had his affection, that I knew him so well.

"And may I say to Mrs. Walter Camp, whom we
love with all our hearts, that we hope her loneliness
and loss may partially be comforted by the thought
that in every part of our country are living those who
have been made better physically and mentally by
Walter's influence and example, and that his departure,
while it has taken him from our sight, has not in any
way lessened the power of his fine spirit in innumerable
lives. There is no other woman in our annals who
more perfectly in her own mind and heart represents
the eternal spirit of Yale; the sister of Yale's greatest
teacher, William Graham Sumner, the wife of Yale's
greatest sportsman, Walter Camp."

And then it was the turn of the gentlest and
most lovable of all sport lovers in America to
speak; a man who in his appearance is bookish
and almost ministerial, but who over a long period
of years has helped to keep the flames of intercollegiate rivalry burning in an orderly fashion,

who served for a time with Walter Camp on the joint athletic committee of Yale and Harvard. Everyone in the chapel knew that Dean LeBaron Russell Briggs of Harvard would remember some unknown and almost quixotic example of Camp's sportsmanship.   For this is a man who takes honor for granted, and who searches in the human spirit for something finer still.   Said Dean Briggs : —

"Walter Camp's preëminence in athletics needs no word of mine.   From ocean to ocean he is known as the father of American football, as the lover and up-holder of all manly sport, as the prophet of physical well-being in the happily efficient life.   I would speak of his personal kindness to one whom he knew but slightly, and whom he rarely or never met except in the delicate relations of intercollegiate athletics.

"From the first moment of our first meeting to the last moment of our last, I found him not honorable merely but singularly friendly and sensitively considerate. On the day of a Princeton–Harvard game, he looked me up at the Pennsylvania Station in New York to discuss some question of athletics.   'Since we are both going to Princeton,' said I, 'why should n't you come with me in the special train for the Harvard team?' 'Your men would n't like that,' he said.   'It would worry them.'   On inquiry I was sorry to learn that he was right.

"What I have told you illustrates perfectly all my experience, official or personal, with Mr. Camp.   For my knowledge of athletics he might well have felt contempt; and athletics was the one subject that brought us together, — scarcely half a dozen times in all. He had a thousand friends whom he knew better; yet here you see him as I saw him, a man not too busy for an act of courtesy hard to surpass in thoughtfulness and grace. To him such acts were but small incidents of a crowded life and possibly soon forgotten. Yet to one man they mean much; and of one man they mean much. There are few stronger searchlights than athletics. I shall never cease to remember with gratitude what the searchlight of athletics revealed to me in Walter Camp."

The last speaker for Yale was President Emeritus Arthur Twining Hadley, for forty years a friend of Walter Camp, and better fitted than any other man to appraise the worth of his service to Yale. He said : —

"During the period of Walter Camp's service as graduate advisor in Athletics, I had the privilege of close association with him in the decision of questions that were often difficult and sometimes grave. Under conditions like these, Walter Camp laid aside his habitual reserve, and let me see what manner of man he was, and how he made himself what he was. In all the matters which came before us, he showed himself not only clear headed but clean minded — anxious to avoid prejudice and unwilling to listen to the idle talk which lies at the root of so many unnecessary quarrels. In this fundamental sense I think he was the cleanest minded man I ever saw. This characteristic was all the more remarkable because Camp was by nature a man of strong feelings and prejudices. He cared for his

friends and wanted them to win. But the very fact
that he cared so much put him on his guard against
anything which might lead him to do his antagonist
less than justice. When David, in one of the noblest
of his Psalms, wished to describe a citizen of Zion, he
used the words 'who taketh not up a reproach against
his neighbor.' To this high standard Walter Camp
measured up squarely and fully. He neither repeated
nor entertained idle gossip. When a suspicion was
unproved he simply said, 'I don't believe it.'

"Even if a fact was proved which seemed to others
to warrant suspicion, he was slow to admit that it
showed any intentional disregard of duty or any fla-
grant want of care. In one grave instance of professionalism which was discovered at another college and
was severely criticized by the press and by the public,
he stood almost alone in believing that there had been
neither evil design nor culpable blindness. 'Every one
of us,' he once said, 'who has to do with the control of
college athletics is sitting on a volcano. We try to
take all the pains we can to keep things clean; but
strive as we may, something may happen to elude us.'

"This habit of self-criticism enabled him to tolerate
the criticisms of others. He was so much afraid that
something might happen which would justly be made
a reproach against us that he did not care greatly for
irresponsible reports about us as long as they were not
true. More than almost any other man I ever knew,
he lived up to the advice offered by St. Paul to the
Corinthians: 'Suffer fools gladly, seeing ye yourselves
are wise.' It was his business to see things as they
were and to keep clear of all prejudice which would

obstruct his vision. If others were less sagacious, that was not his concern.

"And he had much more than this negative freedom from prejudice. He had a positive desire to understand the feelings of others and to put himself in their places. His habit of reserve, to which I have already alluded, sometimes prevented others from seeing how fully he tried to enter into their point of view, but it did not hinder him from understanding them. Deep in his mind, he had at once the craving and the power to know those whom he met.

"I am inclined to think that the possession of this power was his greatest asset in advising Yale teams as to the methods by which they could win, and that it accounted for many things which the public used to attribute to 'Yale Luck.' 'We know what we can do,' he said to me, 'and they know what they can do; but we generally have the advantage of knowing what they can do much better than they know what we can do. They sometimes send scouts to find out something about our plays, but they do not know when we are likely to use a given play because they have never taken the trouble to find out about the psychology of the Yale eleven — how it will react to given conditions.'

"This habit of entering into others' feelings not only made him a good advisor professionally, but a good example outside of his profession. He was the kind of leader which the United States needs to an exceptional degree at the present day. In almost every department of life from politics to literature we are prone to let organized emotion take the place of brains. More than ever we ought to heed the lessons that Walter

Camp's life and work can teach us — to keep our minds so free from prejudice that we may see things clearly; to judge ourselves so critically that we need not fear the misjudgments of our opponents; to enter so intelligently into the real feelings of those with whom we deal that, whether we meet them in coöperation or in honorable strife, we shall know the ground on which we stand and the results we may hope to accomplish."

All sides of Walter Camp's work are mentioned in these tributes: his record as football player and all-around athlete; his success as football coach and football legislator; his public-minded effort to improve the health and fitness of the whole nation. There is nobody else who has done all these things as well as he did.   Above them all, shining clearly in all his acts and in his attitude toward life, was the high, clear flame of sportsmanship; and this, as Dean Briggs pointed out, did not mean honor alone, but generosity and delicacy of spirit.

He had the aristocratic tradition, and he did not let it down.   The great word gentleman, so dangerous when used by anyone not a gentleman, was frequently on his lips.   He dared to rise at student banquets, Professor Phelps informs me, and quote Thackeray's stanza from the poem called "The End of the Play": —

> Who misses or who gains the prize
>   Go, lose or conquer as you can;
> But if you fail or if you rise
>   Be each, pray God, a gentleman.

One has to be very sure of himself to talk in that vein to any group of college men — the quickest audience in the world to puncture pretension or insincerity on the part of a speaker. Camp not only quoted poems before such audiences, and spoke to them about chivalry, but he did some of the best writing of his life on the same subject. Again I must emphasize my belief that too many people think it is "gentlemanly" to lose a game with a smile, and even to make no great effort for victory. Walter Camp fought this delusion, tooth and nail. "A gentleman against a gentleman always plays to win," he wrote. "There is a tacit agreement between them that each shall do his best, and that the best man shall win." Football in his eyes was the modern counterpart of the tourneys of old, the jousts that were marked by a chivalrous spirit but by a keen desire to win. He could not imagine a knight being paid for participation in such tournaments. "No matter how winding the road that eventually brings a dollar from sport into your pocket," he warned, "that dollar is the price of what should be dearer to you than anything else: your honor. If you are enough of a man to be a good athlete and someone asks you to use that athletic ability for gain, don't take money for it, or anything that amounts to pay. A gentleman does not make his living from his athletic prowess. He does not earn anything by his victories except glory and satisfaction. Perhaps the first falling off in this respect began when the laurel wreath became a mug. So long as the mug was but an emblem, and valueless otherwise, there was no harm. There is still no harm where the mug hangs in the room of the winner to indicate his skill; but if the silver mug becomes a silver dollar, let us have the laurel wreath back again."

Observe the sharp, clipped words in which Camp preaches this little sermon. It is addressed, of course, to college athletes and not to professional players — Camp knew most of the first-rate professional athletes, and respected them. But he had no respect for the man who disguised his professionalism. He could not have taught his own type of sportsmanship to such a man, nor could he imagine him bearing himself on the college athletic field with the kind of high chivalry that Camp admired. He admitted that boys could be misguided, and that the boy who took money or its equivalent for playing amateur games was often to be pitied rather than scorned. But his own voice and example was always on the side of absolutely Corinthian sport. All this is easiest to understand when one remembers that Camp was intensely romantic in spirit, and that he had only to close his eyes to see the lists and the barriers where champions rode to unhorse their rivals, with only fame and glory for reward. From those gallent competitions he saved as much romance and courage and glamor as he could, and wove

these qualities into the game of football. His
insistence that the code of honor must be trans-
ferred from the knighthood of old on to the modern
football field was as enduring a contribution to the
development of sport, if a less visible one, as any
of the rules he caused to be enacted for the regulation of the game.

Football became in his hands a game of honor
as well as of pluck, a knightly game as well as a
manly one. And he thought that its spectators
should share this spirit. "A gentleman is courteous," he declared. "It is not courteous to cheer
an error of your opponents. If upon your own
grounds, it is the worst kind of boorishness. So
is any attempt to rattle your opponents by con-
certed cheering and talking. You should cheer any
remarkable plays made by your rivals, and conceal
any chagrin at the loss it may occasion to your
side."

This is a counsel, apparently, of perfection;
but you have only to go from a baseball game to
an intercollegiate football game to realize that
Walter Camp somehow infused into football his
own high generosity of spirit. The cheering for
an opposing team or captain, the restraint that is
shown when an adversary makes a fumble, the
courtesies paid to the opposite side by each college
band — all these are astonishing new phenomena
in athletic sport, and they are all derived directly
from Camp. There is a minority of spectators

who do not understand them ; but their acceptance by the undergraduate and graduate crowds, at least, is very nearly complete.   Never forgetting, or allowing others to forget, that football is a game, Camp nevertheless surrounded it with the most magnanimous traditions that he could teach.   His idea of proper conduct by spectators went very far : —

After winning a match there is no reason why a lot of young men should not do plenty of cheering, but there is every reason why they should not make their enjoyment depend upon insulting those who have lost.   You cannot take your hilarity off into a corner and choke it to death.   But jeers and jibes at the crestfallen mark you as a man who does not know how to bear victory, a man whose pate is addled by excitement, or whose bringing up has been at fault.   When celebrating, do not, I beg of you, do anything because it looks smart. Enjoy yourselves, but do not try to show off.   Don't be tough.   A little unusual hilarity may upon these occasions be overlooked and forgiven, but be ready to appreciate the point beyond which it is carried too far. Show that behind the jolly fun you have the instincts and cultivation of a gentleman's son.   If you find you are losing your head, go home; you will not be sorry for it.

But his final word was to the players of the game — of all college games, great and small : —

I wish I could impress indelibly upon your minds that with you rests the standard of amateur sport.

With no disrespect to any other class or condition, I say that the collegian's standard of purity in sports should be the highest. The very fact that he has leisure to devote four years to a higher education should be taken to involve the duty of acquiring a keener perception of right and wrong in matters where right and wrong depend upon delicacy of honor. Gentlemen do not cheat, nor do they deceive themselves as to what cheating is. If you are the captain of a nine, an eleven, or a crew, read over the rules and notice exactly who are allowed to play as contestants by these rules — not merely by the custom of some predecessor, or of your rival, but by the rules themselves. Having done that, do not let a thought enter your head of using some man not clearly and cleanly eligible. It is your duty to know that every one of your men is straight and square. I know what I am talking about when I say that a college captain can, in ninety-nine cases out of a hundred, know the exact truth about every man he thinks of trying. In investigating and in legislating, remember that what a gentleman wants is fair play, and the best man to win.

Challenges of this kind came from Walter Camp's lips and pen during all his half century in football. With one more characteristic example, we can bring to an end our estimate of what he stood for at Yale: —

It is quite the fashion to say "sentimental bosh" to anyone who preaches such an old-fashioned thing as honor in sport, but among true gentlemen honor is just as real an article as ever, and it can never ring false.

The man who tells you the insufferable rot about being "practical" and discarding sentiment is not the man you should choose as a friend. He will not stand by you in a pinch. When we come to realities, it is only the man who believes in such things as honor that is worth anything. So stick to it, my boy, and keep it bright. Carry it down into the small affairs of school and college.

Far more than athletic success, such an attitude makes an effect on the minds of the men who are exposed to it. And Yale has shown, in full measure and with superb fitness, how much Yale appreciated Walter Camp. The memorial service was the first manifestation of this spirit; notice that it was held on "Monday afternoon in Commencement Week." Such a date in the college year is not a usual one for memorials; Commencement Week is a time for reunions, for gaiety, for the granting of degrees, for the most interesting of the spring sports. But the service was held in that week, and as a result it was possible for many more of Walter Camp's classmates of 1880 to attend, and also a great many men who could not arrange to come to New Haven at another time. The same scrupulous regard for his memory, even at the risk of uprooting tradition, was shown in the choice of the permanent memorial. It was obvious that this should be on Yale Field, and the proposal was made to call the Yale Bowl the Walter Camp Bowl. But that, fine as it would have been, might have limited his memory to football alone. At last it was decided that Yale Field itself should bear his name.

The Yale athletic fields are bisected by Derby Avenue, a main thoroughfare from New Haven. To the north is the Yale Bowl, the Lapham Field House, and the tennis courts; to the south are the baseball diamonds and the running track. Where Derby Avenue separates the north from the south field, it will be widened and will become an ornamental mall. A colonnade, one hundred and ten feet in width and fifty feet in height, designed by John W. Cross, Yale 1900, will be erected at the entrance to the north field, directly in front of the Yale Bowl. The inscription

THE WALTER CAMP
FIELDS

will be cut into the stone over the gateway, and upon the panels on either side will appear the names of the universities and schools that have contributed to this memorial. For it will not be entirely, as at first proposed, the gift of Yale men. Many other men wished to contribute, and Brigadier-General Palmer E. Pierce, president of the National Collegiate Association, named a committee which offered to coöperate with the committee appointed by the Corporation of Yale University. The Yale Committee members are S. Brinckerhoff Thorne, chairman; and William M. Barnum,

Walter Jennings, Vance C. McCormick, George T. Adee, John A. Hartwell, and Artemus L. Gates; with Robert M. Hutchins, secretary. The members of the committee of the N. C. A. A. are Edward K. Hall, chairman; and W. S. Langford of Trinity, Fred W. Moore of Harvard, A. A. Stagg of the University of Chicago, Walter Powell of Wisconsin University, and Robert C. Zuppke of the University of Illinois; together with district chairmen throughout the country, and W. Richmond Smith, of 45 Rose Street, New York, as executive secretary. In the hands of men like these, who knew Walter Camp so intimately, not only is the administration of the fund secure, but it will continue to come from the far-flung graduates and undergraduates of both schools and colleges everywhere. Every boy or man who has been directly or indirectly inspired by Walter Camp will have an opportunity to contribute a small sum to the memorial that will stand as long as athletic sports are played at Yale.

Among all the memorials to great men in the world, there are two which seem particularly appropriate to the place where they stand, and this memorial to Walter Camp is one. The other is a statue on a lonely tropical beach, far from the eyes of the crowd; it represents a man in armor looking out to sea. But the man is Vasco Núñez de Balboa, and the ocean is *his* ocean — the Pacific. Not less impressive, as the years go by, will be this constant reminder of Walter Camp's service, first to the young men of Yale, and then to all the young men in this country. He, too, wore the armor of the high adventurous spirit that dares to strive and to find.

"How often," wrote Grantland Rice in *Collier's Weekly*, "must have come to Walter Camp the memory of old football battles in rain and snow, in sun and shadow — the flying tackle and the savage line thrust — the forward wall braced for the shock — the graceful spiral careening against a sky of blue and gray — the long run down the field — the goal-line stand — the forward pass — the singing and cheering of great crowds — young and old America gathered together on a golden afternoon, with bands playing and banners flying —

"It may have been in the midst of such a dream that the call to quarters came, and Taps was sounded as the great knight came down the field."

APPENDIX A

ALL-AMERICA FOOTBALL TEAMS OF WALTER CAMP

1889

end	Cumnock, Harvard
tackle	Cowan, Princeton
guard	Cranston, Harvard
centre	George, Princeton
guard	Heffelfinger, Yale
tackle	Gill, Yale
end	Stagg, Yale
quarter	Poe, Princeton
halfback	Lee, Harvard
halfback	Channing, Princeton
fullback	Ames, Princeton

1890

Hallowell, Harvard
Newell, Harvard
Riggs, Princeton
Cranston, Harvard
Heffelfinger, Yale
Rhodes, Yale
Warren, Princeton
Dean, Harvard
Corbett, Harvard
McClung, Yale
Homans, Princeton

1891

end	Hinkey, Yale
tackle	Winter, Yale
guard	Heffelfinger, Yale
centre	Adams, Pennsylvania
guard	Riggs, Princeton
tackle	Newell, Harvard
end	Hartwell, Yale
quarter	King, Princeton
halfback	Lake, Harvard
halfback	McClung, Yale
fullback	Homans, Princeton

1892

Hinkey, Yale
Wallis, Yale
Waters, Harvard
Lewis, Harvard
Wheeler, Princeton
Newell, Harvard
Hallowell, Harvard
McCormick, Yale
Brewer, Harvard
King, Princeton
Thayer, Pennsylvania

1893

end	Hinkey, Yale
tackle	Lea, Princeton

1894

Hinkey, Yale
Waters, Harvard

1893 (*Continued*)

guard	Wheeler, Princeton
centre	Lewis, Harvard
guard	Hickok, Yale
tackle	Newell, Harvard
end	Trenchard, Princeton
quarter	King, Princeton
halfback	Brewer, Harvard
halfback	Morse, Princeton
fullback	Butterworth, Yale

1894 (*Continued*)

Wheeler, Princeton
Stillman, Yale
Hickok, Yale
Lea, Princeton
Gelbert, Pennsylvania
Adee, Yale
Knipe, Pennsylvania
Brooke, Pennsylvania
Butterworth, Yale

1895

end	Cabot, Harvard
tackle	Lea, Princeton
guard	Wharton, Pennsylvania
centre	Bull, Pennsylvania
guard	Riggs, Princeton
tackle	Murphy, Yale
end	Gelbert, Pennsylvania
quarter	Wyckoff, Cornell
halfback	Thorne, Yale
halfback	Brewer, Harvard
fullback	Brooke, Pennsylvania

1896

Cabot, Harvard
Church, Princeton
Wharton, Pennsylvania
Gailey, Princeton
Woodruff, Pennsylvania
Murphy, Yale
Gelbert, Pennsylvania
Fincke, Yale
Wrightington, Harvard
Kelly, Princeton
Baird, Princeton

1897

end	Cochran, Princeton
tackle	Chamberlain, Yale
guard	Hare, Pennsylvania
centre	Doucette, Harvard
guard	Brown, Yale
tackle	Outland, Pennsylvania
end	Hall, Yale
quarter	De Saulles, Yale
halfback	Dibblee, Harvard
halfback	Kelly, Princeton
fullback	Minds, Pennsylvania

1898

FIRST TEAM		SECOND TEAM
end	Palmer, Princeton	Poe, Princeton
tackle	Hillebrand, Princeton	Steckle, Michigan
guard	Hare, Pennsylvania	McCracken, Pennsylvania
centre	Overfield, Pennsylvania	Cunningham, Michigan
guard	Brown, Yale	Boal, Harvard
tackle	Chamberlain, Yale	Haughton, Harvard
end	Hallowell, Harvard	Cochran, Harvard
quarter	Daly, Harvard	Kennedy, Chicago
halfback	Outland, Pennsylvania	Richardson, Brown
halfback	Dibblee, Harvard	Warren, Harvard
fullback	Herschberger, Chicago	O'Dea, Wisconsin

THIRD TEAM

end	Folwell, Pennsylvania
tackle	Sweetland, Cornell
guard	Randolph, Penn. State
centre	Jaffray, Harvard
guard	Reed, Cornell
tackle	Foy, West Point
end	Smith, West Point
quarter	Kromer, West Point
halfback	Raymond, Wesleyan
halfback	Benedict, Nebraska
fullback	Romeyn, West Point

1899

FIRST TEAM		SECOND TEAM
end	Campbell, Harvard	Hallowell, Harvard
tackle	Hillebrand, Princeton	Wheelock, Indiana
guard	Hare, Pennsylvania	Edwards, Princeton
centre	Overfield, Pennsylvania	Cunningham, Michigan
guard	Brown, Yale	Wright, Columbia

1899 (*Continued*)

	FIRST TEAM	SECOND TEAM
tackle	Stillman, Yale	Wallace, Pennsylvania
end	Poe, Princeton	Coombs, Pennsylvania
quarter	Daly, Harvard	Kennedy, Chicago
halfback	Seneca, Indians	Richardson, Brown
halfback	McCracken, Pennsylvania	Slaker, Chicago
fullback	McBride, Yale	Wheeler, Princeton

THIRD TEAM

end	Snow, Michigan
tackle	Alexander, Cornell
guard	Trout, Lafayette
centre	Burnett, Harvard
guard	Burden, Harvard
tackle	Pell, Princeton
end	Hamill, Chicago
quarter	Hudson, Indiana
halfback	McLean, Michigan
halfback	Weekes, Columbia
fullback	O'Dea, Wisconsin

1900

	FIRST TEAM	SECOND TEAM
end	Campbell, Harvard	Gould, Yale
tackle	Bloomer, Yale	Wallace, Pennsylvania
guard	Brown, Yale	Wright, Columbia
centre	Olcott, Yale	Sargent, Harvard
guard	Hare, Pennsylvania	Sheldon, Yale
tackle	Stillman, Yale	Lawrence, Harvard
end	Hallowell, Harvard	Coy, Yale
quarter	Fincke, Yale	Daly, Harvard
halfback	Chadwick, Yale	Weekes, Columbia
halfback	Morley, Columbia	Sawin, Harvard
fullback	Hale, Yale	Cure, Lafayette

Third Team

end	Smith, West Point
tackle	Alexander, Cornell
guard	Teas, Pennsylvania
centre	Page, Minnesota
guard	Belknap, Annapolis
tackle	Farnsworth, West Point
end	Van Hoevenberg, Columbia
quarter	Williams, Iowa
halfback	Reiter, Princeton
halfback	Sharpe, Yale
fullback	McCracken, Pennsylvania

1901

	First Team	Second Team
end	Campbell, Harvard	Bowditch, Harvard
tackle	Cutts, Harvard	Blagden, Harvard
guard	Warner, Cornell	Barnard, Harvard
centre	Holt, Yale	Bachman, Lafayette
guard	Lee, Harvard	Hunt, Cornell
tackle	Bunker, West Point	Wheelock, Carlisle
end	Davis, Princeton	Swan, Yale
quarter	Daly, West Point	De Saulles, Yale
halfback	Kernan, Harvard	Purcell, Cornell
halfback	Weekes, Columbia	Ristine, Harvard
fullback	Graydon, Harvard	Cure, Lafayette

Third Team

end	Henry, Princeton
tackle	Pell, Princeton
guard	Olcott, Yale
centre	Fisher, Princeton
guard	Teas, Pennsylvania
tackle	Goss, Yale
end	Gould, Yale
quarter	Johnson, Carlisle

1901 *(Continued)*

THIRD TEAM

halfback	Heston, Michigan
halfback	Morley, Columbia
fullback	Schoelkopf, Cornell

1902

	FIRST TEAM	SECOND TEAM
end	Shevlin, Yale	Sweeley, Michigan
tackle	Hogan, Yale	Pierce, Amherst
guard	De Witt, Princeton	Warner, Cornell
centre	Holt, Yale	Boyers, West Point
guard	Glass, Yale	Goss, Yale
tackle	Kinney, Yale	Knowlton, Harvard
end	Bowditch, Harvard	Davis, Princeton
quarter	Rockwell, Yale	Weeks, Michigan
halfback	Chadwick, Yale	Barry, Brown
halfback	Bunker, West Point	Metcalf, Yale
fullback	Graydon, Harvard	Bowman, Yale

THIRD TEAM

end	Metzgar, Pennsylvania
tackle	Farr, Chicago
guard	Lerum, Wisconsin
centre	McCabe, Pennsylvania
guard	Marshall, Harvard
tackle	Schacht, Minnesota
end	Farmer, Dartmouth
quarter	Daly, West Point
halfback	Foulke, Princeton
halfback	Heston, Michigan
fullback	Torney, West Point

1903

	FIRST TEAM	SECOND TEAM
end	Henry, Princeton	Davis, Princeton
tackle	Hogan, Yale	Thorpe, Columbia
guard	De Witt, Princeton	Riley, West Point
centre	Hooper, Dartmouth	Strathern, Minnesota
guard	A. Marshall, Harvard	Gilman, Dartmouth
tackle	Knowlton, Harvard	Schacht, Minnesota
end	Rafferty, Yale	Shevlin, Yale
quarter	Johnson, Carlisle	Whitman, Dartmouth
halfback	Heston, Michigan	Nichols, Harvard
halfback	Kafer, Princeton	Mitchell, Yale
fullback	Smith, Columbia	R. Miller, Princeton

THIRD TEAM

end	Redden, Michigan
tackle	Turner, Dartmouth
guard	Berthke, Wisconsin
centre	Bruce, Columbia
guard	Piekarski, Pennsylvania
tackle	Maddock, Michigan
end	Rogers, Minnesota
quarter	Harris, Minnesota
halfback	Graver, Michigan
halfback	Stankard, Holy Cross
fullback	Salmon, Notre Dame

1904

	FIRST TEAM	SECOND TEAM
end	Shevlin, Yale	Weede, Pennsylvania
tackle	Cooney, Princeton	Thorpe, Columbia
guard	Piekarski, Pennsylvania	Gilman, Dartmouth
centre	Tipton, West Point	Roraback, Yale
guard	Kinney, Yale	Tripp, Yale
tackle	Hogan, Yale	Curtiss, Michigan
end	Eckersall, Chicago	Gillespie, West Point

1904 (*Continued*)

FIRST TEAM	SECOND TEAM
quarter Stevenson, Pennsylvania	Rockwell, Yale
halfback Hurley, Harvard	Reynolds, Pennsylvania
halfback Heston, Michigan	Hubbard, Amherst
fullback Smith, Pennsylvania	Mills, Harvard

THIRD TEAM

end	Glaze, Dartmouth
tackle	Butkiewicz, Pennsylvania
guard	Short, Princeton
centre	Torrey, Pennsylvania
guard	Thorpe, Minnesota
tackle	Doe, West Point
end	Rothgeb, Illinois
quarter	Harris, Minnesota
halfback	Hoyt, Yale
halfback	Vaughn, Dartmouth
fullback	Bender, Nebraska

1905

	FIRST TEAM	SECOND TEAM
end	Shevlin, Yale	Catlin, Chicago
tackle	Lamson, Pennsylvania	Forbes, Yale
guard	Tripp, Yale	Thompson, Cornell
centre	Torrey, Pennsylvania	Flanders, Yale
guard	Burr, Harvard	Schulte, Michigan
tackle	Squires, Harvard	Curtiss, Michigan
end	Glaze, Dartmouth	Marshall, Minnesota
quarter	Eckersall, Chicago	Hutchinson, Yale
halfback	Roome, Yale	Morse, Yale
halfback	Hubbard, Amherst	Sheble, Pennsylvania
fullback	McCormick, Princeton	Van Saltza, Columbia

THIRD TEAM

end	Levine, Pennsylvania
tackle	Berthke, Wisconsin
guard	Fletcher, Brown
centre	Gale, Chicago
guard	Maxwell, Swarthmore
tackle	Biglow, Yale
end	Tooker, Princeton
quarter	Crowell, Swarthmore
halfback	Hammond, Michigan
halfback	Findlay, Wisconsin
fullback	Bedeck, Chicago

1906

	FIRST TEAM	SECOND TEAM
ena	Forbes, Yale	Dague, Annapolis
tackle	Biglow, Yale	Draper, Pennsylvania
guard	Burr, Harvard	Ziegler, Pennsylvania
centre	Dunn, Penn. State	Hockenberger, Yale
guard	Thompson, Cornell	Dillon, Princeton
tackle	Cooney, Princeton	Osborn, Harvard
end	Wister, Princeton	Marshall, Minnesota
quarter	Eckersall, Chicago	Jones, Yale
halfback	Mayhew, Brown	Hollenback, Pennsylvania
halfback	Knox, Yale	Wendell, Harvard
fullback	Veeder, Yale	McCormick, Princeton

THIRD TEAM

end	Levine, Pennsylvania
tackle	Weeks, West Point
guard	Kersberg, Harvard
centre	Hunt, Indians
guard	Christy, West Point
tackle	Northcroft, Annapolis
end	Exendine, Carlisle

1906 *(Continued)*

THIRD TEAM

quarter	E. Dillon, Princeton
halfback	Morse, Yale
halfback	Manier, Vanderbilt
fullback	Garrels, Michigan

1907

	FIRST TEAM	SECOND TEAM
end	Dague, Annapolis	Exendine, Carlisle
tackle	Draper, Pennsylvania	Horr, Syracuse
guard	Ziegler, Pennsylvania	Rich, Dartmouth
centre	Schulz, Michigan	Grant, Harvard
guard	Erwin, West Point	Thompson, Cornell
tackle	Biglow, Yale	O'Rourke, Cornell
end	Alcott, Yale	Scarlett, Pennsylvania
quarter	Jones, Yale	Dillon, Princeton
halfback	Wendell, Harvard	Marks, Dartmouth
halfback	Harlan, Princeton	Hollenback, Pennsylvania
fullback	McCormick, Princeton	Coy, Yale

THIRD TEAM

end	Wister, Princeton
tackle	Lang, Dartmouth
guard	Goebel, Yale
centre	Phillips, Princeton
guard	Krider, Swarthmore
tackle	Weeks, West Point
end	McDonald, Harvard
quarter	Steffen, Chicago
halfback	Capron, Minnesota
halfback	Houser, Carlisle
fullback	Douglas, Annapolis

1908

	FIRST TEAM	SECOND TEAM
end	Scarlett, Pennsylvania	Dennie, Brown
tackle	Fish, Harvard	Siegling, Princeton
guard	Goebel, Yale	Andrus, Yale
centre	Nourse, Harvard	Philoon, West Point
guard	Tobin, Dartmouth	Messmer, Wisconsin
tackle	Horr, Syracuse	O'Rourke, Cornell
end	Schilmiller, Dartmouth	Reifsnider, Annapolis
quarter	Steffen, Chicago	Cutler, Harvard
halfback	Tibbott, Princeton	Ver Wiebe, Harvard
halfback	Hollenback, Pennsyl-	Mayhew, Brown
	vania	Walder, Cornell
fullback	Coy, Yale	

THIRD TEAM

end	Page, Chicago
tackle	Draper, Pennsylvania
guard	Van Hook, Illinois
centre	Brusse, Dartmouth
guard	Hoar, Harvard
tackle	Northcroft, Annapolis
end	Johnson, West Point
quarter	Miller, Pennsylvania
halfback	Thorpe, Carlisle
halfback	Gray, Amherst
fullback	McCaa, Lafayette

1909

	FIRST TEAM	SECOND TEAM
end	Regnier, Brown	Bankhart, Dartmouth
tackle	Fish, Harvard	Lilley, Yale
guard	Benbrook, Michigan	Goebel, Yale
centre	Cooney, Yale	P. Withington, Harvard
guard	Andrus, Yale	Tobin, Dartmouth

1909 (*Continued*)

FIRST TEAM		SECOND TEAM
tackle	Hobbs, Yale	McKay, Harvard
end	Kilpatrick, Yale	Braddock, Pennsylvania
quarter	McGovern, Minnesota	Howe, Yale
halfback	Philbin, Yale	Allerdice, Michigan
halfback	Minot, Harvard	Magidsohn, Michigan
fullback	Coy, Yale	Marks, Dartmouth

THIRD TEAM

end	Page, Chicago
tackle	Siegling, Princeton
guard	L. Withington, Harvard
centre	Farnum, Minnesota
guard	Fisher, Harvard
tackle	Casey, Michigan
end	McCaffrey, Fordham
quarter	Sprackling, Brown
halfback	Corbett, Harvard
halfback	Miller, Notre Dame
fullback	McCaa, Lafayette

1910

FIRST TEAM		SECOND TEAM
end	Kilpatrick, Yale	(No selection)
tackle	McKay, Harvard	
guard	Benbrook, Michigan	
centre	Cozens, Pennsylvania	
guard	Fisher, Harvard	
tackle	Walker, Minnesota	
end	Wells, Michigan	
quarter	Sprackling, Brown	
halfback	Wendell, Harvard	
halfback	Pendleton, Princeton	
fullback	Mercer, Pennsylvania	

Third Team

(No selection)

1911

	First Team	Second Team
end	White, Princeton	Smith, Harvard
tackle	Hart, Princeton	Munk, Cornell
guard	Fisher, Harvard	Scruby, Chicago
centre	Ketcham, Yale	Bluthenthal, Princeton
guard	Duff, Princeton	McDevitt, Yale
tackle	Devore, West Point	Scully, Yale
end	Bomeisler, Yale	Very, Penn. State
quarter	Howe, Yale	Sprackling, Brown
halfback	Wendell, Harvard	Morey, Dartmouth
halfback	Thorpe, Carlisle	Camp, Yale
fullback	Dalton, Annapolis	Rosenwald, Minnesota

Third Team

end	Ashbaugh, Brown
tackle	Buser, Wisconsin
guard	Francis, Yale
centre	Weems, Annapolis
guard	Arnold, West Point
tackle	Brown, Annapolis
end	Kallett, Syracuse
quarter	Capron, Minnesota
halfback	Mercer, Pennsylvania
halfback	Wells, Michigan
fullback	Hudson, Trinity

1912

	First Team	Second Team
end	Felton, Harvard	Very, Penn. State
tackle	Englehorn, Dartmouth	Probst, Syracuse

1912 (*Continued*)

	FIRST TEAM	SECOND TEAM
guard	Pennock, Harvard	Cooney, Yale
centre	Ketcham, Yale	Parmenter, Harvard
guard	Logan, Princeton	Kulp, Brown
tackle	Butler, Wisconsin	Trickey, Iowa
end	Bomeisler, Yale	Hoeffel, Wisconsin
quarter	Crowther, Brown	Pazzetti, Lehigh
halfback	Brickley, Harvard	Morey, Dartmouth
halfback	Thorpe, Carlisle	Norgren, Chicago
fullback	Mercer, Pennsylvania	Wendell, Harvard

THIRD TEAM

end	Ashbaugh, Brown
tackle	Shaughnessy, Minnesota
guard	Bennett, Dartmouth
centre	Bluthenthal, Princeton
guard	Brown, Annapolis
tackle	Devore, West Point
end	Jordan, Bucknell
quarter	Bacon, Wesleyan
halfback	Hardage, Vanderbilt
halfback	Baker, Princeton
fullback	Pumpelly, Yale

1913

	FIRST TEAM	SECOND TEAM
end	Hogsett, Dartmouth	Fritz, Cornell
tackle	Ballin, Princeton	Butler, Wisconsin
guard	Pennock, Harvard	Busch, Carlisle
centre	Des Jardiens, Chicago	Marting, Yale
guard	Brown, Annapolis	Ketcham, Yale
tackle	Talbot, Yale	Weyand, West Point
end	Merrilat, West Point	Hardwick, Harvard
quarter	Huntington, Colgate	Wilson, Yale
halfback	Craig, Michigan	Spiegel, Wash. and Jeff.
halfback	Brickley, Harvard	Guyon, Carlisle
fullback	Mahan, Harvard	Eichenlaub, Notre Dame

THIRD TEAM

end	Solon, Minnesota
tackle	Halligan, Nebraska
guard	Munns, Cornell
centre	Paterson, Michigan
guard	Talman, Rutgers
tackle	Storer, Harvard
end	Rockne, Notre Dame
quarter	Miller, Penn. State
halfback	Baker, Princeton
halfback	Norgren, Chicago
fullback	Whitney, Dartmouth

1914

	FIRST TEAM	SECOND TEAM
end	Hardwick, Harvard	Merrilat, West Point
tackle	Ballin, Princeton	Nash, Rutgers
guard	Pennock, Harvard	Jordan, Texas
centre	McEwan, West Point	Des Jardiens, Chicago
guard	Chapman, Illinois	Shenk, Princeton
tackle	Trumbull, Harvard	Patterson, Wash. and Jeff.
end	O'Hearn, Cornell	Brann, Yale
quarter	Ghee, Dartmouth	Barrett, Cornell
halfback	Maulbetsch, Michigan	Spiegel, Wash. and Jeff.
halfback	Bradlee, Harvard	Cahall, Lehigh
fullback	Mahan, Harvard	LeGore, Yale

THIRD TEAM

end	Solon, Minnesota
tackle	Halligan, Nebraska
guard	Spears, Dartmouth
centre	Cruikshank, Wash. and Jeff.
guard	Meacham, West Point
tackle	Weyand, West Point
end	Overesch, Annapolis

1914 (*Continued*)

THIRD TEAM

quarter	Wilson, Yale
halfback	Pogue, Illinois
halfback	Talman, Rutgers
fullback	Whitney, Dartmouth

1915

	FIRST TEAM	SECOND TEAM
end	Baston, Minnesota	Herron, Pittsburgh
tackle	Gilman, Harvard	Buck, Wisconsin
guard	Spears, Dartmouth	Hogg, Princeton
centre	Peck, Pittsburgh	Cool, Cornell
guard	Schlachter, Syracuse	Black, Yale
tackle	Abell, Colgate	Vandergraaf, Alabama
end	Shelton, Cornell	Higgins, Penn. State
quarter	Barrett, Cornell	Watson, Harvard
halfback	King, Harvard	Tibbott, Princeton
halfback	Macomber, Illinois	Oliphant, West Point
fullback	Mahan, Harvard	Talman, Rutgers

THIRD TEAM

end	Heyman, Wash. and Jeff.
tackle	Cody, Vanderbilt
guard	Dadmun, Harvard
centre	McEwan, West Point
guard	Taylor, Auburn
tackle	Halligan, Nebraska
end	Squier, Illinois
quarter	Russell, Chicago
halfback	Abraham, Oregon Aggies
halfback	Mayer, Virginia
fullback	Berryman, Penn. State

1916

	FIRST TEAM	SECOND TEAM
end	Baston, Minnesota	Herron, Pittsburgh
tackle	West, Colgate	Ward, Annapolis
guard	Black, Yale	Hogg, Princeton
centre	Peck, Pittsburgh	McEwan, West Point
guard	Dadmun, Harvard	Backman, Notre Dame
tackle	Horning, Colgate	Gates, Yale
end	Moseley, Yale	Miller, Pennsylvania
quarter	Anderson, Colgate	Purdy, Brown
halfback	Oliphant, West Point	LeGore, Yale
halfback	Pollard, Brown	Casey, Harvard
fullback	Harley, Ohio State	Berry, Pennsylvania

THIRD TEAM

end	Coolidge, Harvard
tackle	Beckett, Oregon
guard	Garrett, Rutgers
centre	Phillips, Georgia Tech.
guard	Seagraves, Washington
tackle	Ignico, Wash. and Jeff.
end	Vowell, Tennessee
quarter	Curry, Vanderbilt
halfback	Gilroy, Georgetown
halfback	Driscoll, Northwestern
fullback	McCreight, Wash. and Jeff.

In 1917, owing to American participation in the World War, Walter Camp did not make an All-America football selection. In 1918, with the United States at war, Walter Camp did not choose a collegiate All-America football team, but chose a Service All-America team from the training camps. College and military training camps are shown.

1918   Service Team

	FIRST TEAM	SECOND TEAM
end	Rasmussen, Nebraska Grant	Ellenberger, Cornell Dix
tackle	Beckett, Oregon Mare Island	Moriarty Coast Naval Reserve
guard	Black, Yale Newport Reserve	Thurman, Virginia Jackson
centre	Callahan, Yale Newport Reserve	Hommand, Kansas Funston
guard	Allendinger, Michigan Fort Sheridan	Withington, Harvard Funston
tackle	West, Colgate Dix	Blacklock, Michigan Aggy Great Lakes
end	Gardiner, Carlisle Custer	Mitchell Mare Island Marines
quarter	Watkins, Colgate Mineola	Anderson, Colgate Dix
halfback	Casey, Harvard Boston Navy Yard	Shiverick, Cornell Grant
halfback	Minot, Harvard Devens	Barrett, Cornell Newport Reserves
fullback	Smith, Michigan Great Lakes	Maxfield, Lafayette Fort Slocum

THIRD TEAM

end	Dennit, Brown Funston
tackle	Robertson, Dartmouth Dodge
guard	Snyder, 91st Division Lewis
centre	White, Yale Jackson
guard	Holder, 91st Division Lewis

tackle	Lathrop, Notre Dame
	Grant
end	Hunt
	Coast Naval Reserve
quarter	Costello, Georgetown
	Custer
halfback	O'Boyle, Georgetown
	Pelham
halfback	Blair, Maryland
	Upton
fullback	Thayer, Pennsylvania
	Meade

Walter Camp noted in his selection that he had not included West Point and Annapolis; and that some of the teams of Southern training camps had not finished their season when he made his choices, and so were not considered.

1919

	FIRST TEAM	SECOND TEAM
end	Higgins, Penn. State	Weston, Wisconsin
tackle	West, Colgate	Ingwersen, Illinois
guard	Alexander, Syracuse	Denfield, Annapolis
centre	Weaver, Center	Bailey, West Virginia
guard	Youngstrom, Dartmouth	Depler, Illinois
tackle	Henry, Wash. and Jeff.	Grimm, Washington
end	H. Miller, Pennsylvania	Dumoe, Lafayette
quarter	McMillin, Center	Strubing, Princeton
halfback	Casey, Harvard	Trimble, Princeton
halfback	Harley, Ohio State	Oss, Minnesota
fullback	Rodgers, West Virginia	Braden, Yale

THIRD TEAM

end	Blaik, West Point
tackle	Slater, Iowa
guard	Clark, Harvard
centre	Callahan, Yale

1919 (*Continued*)

THIRD TEAM

guard	Pixley, Ohio State
tackle	Cody, Vanderbilt
end	Roberts, Center
quarter	Boynton, Williams
halfback	Steers, Oregon
halfback	Gillo, Colgate
fullback	Robertson, Dartmouth

1920

	FIRST TEAM	SECOND TEAM
end	Carney, Illinois	Urban, Boston College
tackle	Keck, Princeton	Goetz, Michigan
guard	Callahan, Yale	Wilkie, Annapolis
centre	Stein, Pittsburgh	Cunningham, Dartmouth
guard	Woods, Harvard	Alexander, Syracuse
tackle	Scott, Wisconsin	McMillan, California
end	Fincher, Georgia Tech.	LeGendre, Princeton
quarter	Lourie, Princeton	McMillin, Center
halfback	Stinchcomb,Ohio State	Garrity, Princeton
halfback	Way, Penn. State	Davies, Pittsburgh
fullback	Gipp, Notre Dame	French, West Point

THIRD TEAM

end	Ewen, Annapolis
tackle	Voss, Detroit
guard	Breidster, West Point
centre	Havemeyer, Harvard
guard	Trott, Ohio State
tackle	Dickens, Yale
end	Muller, California
quarter	Boynton, Williams
halfback	Haines, Penn. State
halfback	Leech, Virginia Military Institute
fullback	Horween, Harvard

1921

FIRST TEAM		SECOND TEAM
end	Muller, California	Swanson, Nebraska
tackle	Stein, Wash. and Jeff.	Slater, Iowa
guard	Schwab, Lafayette	Trott, Ohio State
centre	Vick, Michigan	Larsen, Annapolis
guard	Brown, Harvard	Bedenk, Penn. State
tackle	McGuire, Chicago	Keck, Princeton
end	Roberts, Center	Kiley, Notre Dame
quarter	A. Devine, Iowa	McMillin, Center
halfback	Killinger, Penn. State	Owen, Harvard
halfback	Aldrich, Yale	Davies, Pittsburgh
fullback	Kaw, Cornell	Mohardt, Notre Dame

THIRD TEAM

end	Crisler, Chicago
tackle	Into, Yale
guard	Pucelik, Nebraska
centre	Stein, Pittsburgh
guard	Whelchel, Georgia
tackle	McMillan, California
end	Stephens, California
quarter	Lourie, Princeton
halfback	French, West Point
halfback	Barchet, Annapolis
fullback	Barron, Georgia Tech.

1922

FIRST TEAM		SECOND TEAM
end	Taylor, Annapolis	Kirk, Michigan
tackle	Treat, Princeton	Waldorf, Syracuse
guard	Schwab, Lafayette	Cross, Yale
centre	Garbisch, West Point	Bowser, Pittsburgh
guard	Hubbard, Harvard	Setron, West Virginia
tackle	Thurman, Pennsylvania	Neidlinger, Dartmouth

1922 (*Continued*)

FIRST TEAM	SECOND TEAM
end Muller, California	Bomar, Vanderbilt
quarter Locke, Iowa	Smythe, West Point
halfback Kaw, Cornell	Morrison, California
halfback Kipke, Michigan	Owen, Harvard
fullback John Thomas, Chicago	Barron, Georgia Tech.

THIRD TEAM

end	Kopf, Wash. and Jeff.
tackle,	Below, Wisconsin
guard	McMillen, Illinois
centre	Peterson, Nebraska
guard	Dickinson, Princeton
tackle	Gulian, Brown
end	Kadesky, Iowa
quarter	Uteritz, Michigan
halfback	Jordan, Yale
halfback	Barchet, Annapolis
fullback	Castner, Notre Dame

1923

FIRST TEAM	SECOND TEAM
end Bomar, Vanderbilt	McRae, Syracuse
tackle Milstead, Yale	Wiederquist, Wash. and Jeff.
guard Hubbard, Harvard	Brown, Notre Dame
centre Blott, Michigan	Lovejoy, Yale
guard Bedenk, Penn. State	Aschenbach, Dartmouth
tackle Sundstrom, Cornell	Deibel, Lafayette
end Hazel, Rutgers	Tallman, West Virginia
quarter Pfann, Cornell	Richeson, Yale
halfback Grange, Illinois	Wilson, Penn. State
halfback Martineau, Minnesota	Tryon, Colgate
fullback Mallory, Yale	Stevens, Yale

THIRD TEAM

end	Stout, Princeton
tackle	Beam, California
guard	Carney, Annapolis
centre	Garbisch, West Point
guard	Johnson, Texas A. and M.
tackle	Bassett, Nebraska
end	Luman, Yale
quarter	Dunn, Marquette
halfback	Koppish, Columbia
halfback	Bohren, Pittsburgh
fullback	Nevers, Stanford

1924

	FIRST TEAM	SECOND TEAM
end	Bjorkman, Dartmouth	Wakefield, Vanderbilt
tackle	McGinley, Pennsylvania	Beattie, Princeton
guard	Slaughter, Michigan	Abramson, Minnesota
centre	Garbisch, West Point	Lovejoy, Yale
guard	Horrell, California	Pondelik, Chicago
tackle	Weir, Nebraska	Waldorf, Syracuse
end	Berry, Lafayette	Lawson, Stamford
quarter	Stuhldreher, Notre Dame	Slagle, Princeton
		Pond, Yale
halfback	Grange, Illinois	Wilson, Univer. of Wash.
halfback	Koppisch, Columbia	Crowley, Notre Dame
fullback	Hazel, Rutgers	

THIRD TEAM

end	Mahaney, Holy Cross
tackle	Wissinger, Pittsburgh
guard	Fleckenstein, Iowa
centre	Walsh, Notre Dame
guard	Mahan, West Virginia
tackle	Gowdy, Chicago

1924 *(Continued)*

THIRD TEAM

end   Frazer, West Point
quarter   Stivers, Idaho
halfback   Imlay, California
halfback   Keefer, Brown
fullback   Strader, St. Mary's

APPENDIX B

THE DAILY DOZEN

The words "Daily Dozen" have come into such common use that many people are now doing curious physical exercises of their own devising — or which they dimly remember from their schooldays — and say proudly that they are doing the Daily Dozen. They are not. The words apply to only one simple and easily learned system of movements. There is no apparatus; no dumbbells or wands or chest weights or medicine ball; nothing to buy, and no more space necessary than you have in your bedroom.

— WALTER CAMP

In his book, *The Daily Dozen*, published by the Reynolds Publishing Company, Inc., New York City, from which the quotation that follows is made by permission, Walter Camp makes certain suggestions that will make the Daily Dozen more effective. To a young man or woman, cramped and confined by indoor life, he recommends the Daily Dozen once in the morning, once at noon, and once at night. To older people, he recommends this exercise only once a day. His specific advice on the different movements is, in part, as follows: —

THE DAILY DOZEN

1. Hands: This exercise, and the next two, are chiefly for use in groups, with a leader. At the command "hands," stand erect, arms hanging at sides, heels slightly separated, feet pointed straight ahead.

2. Hips: Without changing position of body, place hands on hips, thumbs pointing to the rear, fingers extended. This motion should be made easily, without the stiffness of military drill.

3. Head: Bring both arms up, bracing elbows to the rear and allow the tips of the fingers to meet at the back of the head. If you are directing a class, vary the order of these three exercises.

7. Crawl: "Cross" position. Raise left arm, and let the right hand crawl slowly down toward right knee, curving left arm over head, until fingers touch right side of neck. Resume "cross" position. Then reverse these arm movements. Repeat ten times.

8. Curl: "Cross" position, feet 18 inches apart. Clench fists, lower arms (inhaling) and bend slowly forward until fists come under arm pits, head and shoulders back. Loosen hands, and push straight forward (exhaling). Then bend forward from waist, letting hands come back across hips and raise them behind you. Begin to inhale again as you return to "cross" position, ready to repeat. Ten times.

9. Crouch: "Cross" position, feet 18 inches apart. Rise on toes; keep arms out. Squat slowly down as far as you can, inhaling. Come up slowly, exhaling, and letting heels touch floor as you rise. Five times.

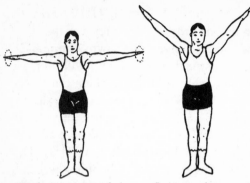

4. Grind: Arms outstretched straight from shoulders. This is called the " cross " position. Keeping the arms stiff, turn the palms upward and make six-inch circles with hands, five times forward, five backward.

5. Grate: Arms at " cross " position, palms down. Lift arms very slowly to angle of about forty-five degrees (inhaling). Bring them down slowly to shoulder level (exhaling). Repeat ten times.

6. Grasp: Stand at "head" position. Keeping neck bent back, incline body forward (exhaling). Straighten slowly (inhaling) to first position, then bend backward as far as possible. Repeat ten times.

10. Wave: "Cross" position. Raise arms and lock fingers above head. Snap arms against head. Moving only from waist, make a circle with your clasped hands extended above your head. Repeat five times in each direction.

11. Weave: "Cross" position, feet apart. Raise right arm, keeping eyes on it as it goes up; bend left knee and lower left arm until fingers touch floor, between feet. Come back slowly to "cross" position and reverse. Five times for each hand.

12. Wing: "Cross" position. Exhale, bringing arms straight before you. Swing arms down and back, bending forward slowly from waist. Keep head up, eyes forward. Go back slowly to "cross" position, inhaling, and raise arms straight up over head. Ten times.

The first three exercises, HANDS, HIPS, HEAD, were devised for use in groups, but they can be used also by the individual under his own commands. They are excellent postural motions, and will increase muscular control. Go through each of them ten times. At "HANDS," the fingers should be on the thighs, the arms straight down and nearly, but not quite, fully extended. At "HIPS," the hands should be placed as in the illustration, with the elbows back. At "HEAD," touch the tips of the fingers together behind the head, with eyes facing straight to the front, chin brought slightly in, and the elbows kept back. When you bring the hands down, they should be under control and not flop down.

In the "GRIND," turn the palms of the hands squarely upward, and keep the shoulders back; make the motion almost entirely from the shoulders, and feel that you are lifting, as it were, and lifting slowly so that the effort is felt in the muscles of the shoulders.

In the "GRATE," the arms should be lifted from the shoulders with the backs of the hands upward, and elevated at an angle of exactly forty-five degrees.

In the "GRASP," pay particular attention to keeping the head up as the body goes forward. Keep your eyes fixed throughout on a point directly ahead of them. Exhale while the body is going forward and inhale as it rises. In going forward, the movement should be very slight, just enough to secure the slight pull on the abdominal muscles, without putting any strain on them.

In the "CRAWL," the motion is largely made just above the hips (like the pivot in golf). The hand that rests on the thigh should slide down while the other curls over the head. In the "CURL," head and shoulders should go slightly back as the fists are brought into the armpits. Take a full inhalation as this motion is made, and then exhale slightly as the hands are put out in front and then swept down past the hips and up behind the body. When this final position is reached, inhalation begins slowly in order to reach its maximum when the body is once more erect. In the "CROUCH," it is good practice after complete control has been acquired to balance in the lowered position, while moving slightly from side to side. This will still further strengthen the arches of the feet.

In the "WAVE," no extreme motions are desirable; the more closely the arms are kept to the ears, the more effective is this movement. In the "WEAVE," keep the extended arms in line with the shoulder turning the body, and letting the forward hand touch midway between the feet. In the "WING," pay particular attention to getting the breathing rhythmic; exhaling as the body goes down and inhaling as it comes up.

Each of these movements has its own particular province; among them, they cover the entire muscular circuit. The "GRIND" flattens down projecting shoulder blades, at the same time expanding the chest. The "GRATE" puts a muscular cap over the shoulder, which greatly improves its appearance. The "GRASP" strengthens the muscles at the back of the neck, giving better poise to the head which often relieves eyestrain. The "CRAWL" tends to massage the middle section of the body. The "CURL" is a breathing exercise and also improves the muscles of the back. The

"CROUCH" greatly improves control of the back muscles so vital in all outdoor games, and strengthens the arches of the feet. The "WAVE" strengthens the muscles of the sides, and tends to reduce any excess weight at the waist. The "WEAVE" gives particular work to the muscles of the back, and even more than the "WAVE" it tends to take off excess fat around the waist. Finally, the "WING" tends to make the breathing more rhythmic without conscious effort, at the same time giving a certain amount of muscular improvement at the shoulders and back. When special results are desired, the use of any particular movement may be increased.